Sacred Companions

The Gift of Spiritual Friendship & Direction

DAVID G. BENNER

Foreword by Larry Crabb

InterVarsity Press
Downers Grove, Illinois

InterVarsity Press
P.O. Box 1400, Downers Grove, IL 60515-1426
World Wide Web: www.ivpress.com
E-mail: mail@ivpress.com

InterVarsity Press® is the book-publishing division of InterVarsity Christian Fellowship/USA®,
a student movement active on campus at hundreds of universities, colleges and schools of
nursing in the United States of America, and a member movement of the International
Fellowship of Evangelical Students. For information about local and regional activities, write
Public Relations Dept., InterVarsity Christian Fellowship/USA, 6400 Schroeder Rd., P.O. Box
7895, Madison, WI 53707-7895, or visit the IVCF website at <www.ivcf.org>.

Scripture quotations, unless otherwise noted, are taken from the Jerusalem Bible (JB),
copyright © 1966 by Darton, Longman & Todd, Ltd., and Doubleday & Company, Inc.
All rights reserved.

While all of the stories and examples in this book are based on real people and events, some
names and identifying details have been altered to protect the privacy of the individuals
involved. Some illustrations are composites of different persons and situations.

Cover photograph: © Robert Buelteman

ISBN 0-8308-2342-5

Printed in the United States of America ∞

Library of Congress Cataloging-in-Publication Data

Benner, David G.
    Sacred companions: the gift of spiritual friendship and direction / David G. Benner.
       p.cm.
    Includes bibliographical references.
    ISBN 0-8308-2342-5 (cloth: alk. paper)
       1. Friendship—Religious aspects—Christianity. 2. Spiritual direction. I. Title.
    BV4647.F7 B46 2002
    253.5'3—dc21

                                                                2001051939

P   17   16   15   14   13   12   11   10   9   8   7   6   5   4   3   2   1

Y   15   14   13   12   11   10   09   08   07   06   05   04   03   02

To
Rev. Robert W. Harvey
(1931-2000)
much-loved sacred companion
to so many of us

Contents

Foreword

When I'm still, I sometimes can feel a gentle breeze blowing softly into my soul. Others are reporting the same experience.

I am excited. For this stubborn melancholic to sense excitement stirring, something supernatural must be going on. I believe it is.

In my nearly fifty years of living as a Christian, I have never seen the soul's thirst for God more talked about, more recognized as a vital motivation in the human personality or more strongly experienced as a consuming passion. Perhaps a revolution is under way, a revolution of the Spirit that is about to shift our core energies *away from* arranging life to make it as satisfying as possible *to* drawing near to God.

The spiritual climate is ripe. Jesus seekers across the world are being prepared to abandon the old way of the written code for the new way of the Spirit. Paul told us long ago we've been freed by the gospel to live a new way, but we've not known what it is or how to do it.

But now, living on this fallen planet in these jars of clay has disillusioned us to the point where maybe we're willing to give up trying to do what's right so that life will work. It just isn't happening, at least not reliably. No amount of effort, including good "Christian" effort, makes life always go as we want. Even when it does, when things do go our way, our souls at best are half filled. Something that was missing when blessings were absent remains missing in their presence.

More people are open as never before to letting painful hardships and empty pleasures drive us to chasing after God's own heart, to doing whatever it takes to know God and to see Christ formed in us. We're beginning to wonder what else really matters.

In my judgment nothing is more needed in advancing this revolution than making the idea of spiritual direction more biblically rooted and clearly understandable (insofar as mystery can be understood) and making the wise practice of spiritual direction more valued and common. In the past year alone I have read a couple of dozen books on this topic. I'm grateful for them all.

But one book stands above the others as simple enough to be profound, illustrative enough to demystify the process while allowing it to remain supernatural, and passionate enough to steer us away from a merely academic approach to spiritual direction. That book, of course, is the one you're now holding.

I've known David Benner for many years, both by reputation and writing. From a distance I have long respected Dr. Benner as a perceptive thinker and a seriously *Christian* psychologist in every sense of the word.

But now I know David. In the past year he and I have become friends. Our hearts are meeting as we realize we are walking a similar journey. My respect has deepened and an experience of fellowship in the gospel has begun.

From knowing him, I could have endorsed this book without even reading it. But I have read it—several times. And I assigned it as the lead book in the first class I ever taught on spiritual direction. I think it's that good.

Read it slowly. Read it several times. Read it with a notepad beside you and a pen poised to record your thoughts and impressions. If you do, by the time you finish I am quite certain at least three things will happen: (1) you'll be more aware of your thirst to know God, (2) you'll pray earnestly for someone to provide you with spiritual direction, and (3) you'll ask God for the privilege of offering it to others.

Readers of this book by David Benner will, I predict, feel the fresh wind of the Spirit blowing into and through their souls. They will be better equipped to join the revolution of leaving the old way behind, the way of living comfortably in this world. And they will more deeply yearn to live the new way of seeking God and living for him in this disappointing world until they wake up in the next one, where eternal satisfaction is guaranteed.

Larry Crabb

Preface

Companions on the Spiritual Journey

Of all the social changes in the last several decades, nothing has surprised me more than the recent rise of interest in spirituality. For many in Western societies, a hunger for the sacred has emerged out of the bankruptcy of materialism and secularism. And for many in the church, a longing for a deep encounter with God has arisen out of the arid soil of knowing about God but having little personal, experiential knowing of him.

My world is full of people on a spiritual journey—cradle Roman Catholics rediscovering their church and faith, former atheists visiting aboriginal healing circles, Christians practicing Buddhist meditation, new age seekers pursuing encounters with the sacred, evangelicals discovering mysticism, Roman Catholics discovering Bible study and intercessory prayer, and Protestants discovering liturgy and the sacraments.

Lunch hours in the public mental health clinic where I work used to be filled with the usual topics of conversation—gossip, weekend activities and plans, sports and entertainment. Now the number-one topic is often spirituality. (The number two remains clinic gossip!) People seem to be bursting to tell anyone who will listen about their spiritual quest. They long to share their journey with others. They want people who not only will listen to them but can relate to their story because they are on a spiritual journey of their own.

Spirituality means different things to these people. But a common component of those diverse meanings is the notion of being connected. These people all long to be connected—to God (however he/she/it is understood), to others, to themselves and often to the earth.

The hunger for connection is one of the most fundamental desires of the human heart. We are like immigrants in a new land, with no family or friends and no sense of place. We seem to have lost our mooring. Or perhaps we have lost some part of ourselves. Like pieces of a puzzle seeking their adjoining pieces, we long for connections that will assure us that we belong.

But it is not just connections in general that we seek. In the core of our being we yearn for intimacy. We want people to share our lives. We want soul friends. We were never intended to make the life pilgrimage alone. And attempting to make the spiritual journey on our own is particularly hazardous.

Paradoxically, however, what we most deeply long for we also fear. How else can we explain our reluctance to be genuinely known by those with whom we are most intimate? Often it seems that what we want is the fruit of companionship without the demands of genuine intimacy. Yet something within us remains dissatisfied with the safe but superficial relationships we experience. Our souls ache for a place of deep encounter with others. Our fears may partially mask this ache, but it won't go away. We want companions for the journey, companions with whom we can share our soul and our journey.

Defining Our Terms

I have mentioned the ambiguity of the term *spirituality*. But now I have introduced another equally ambiguous term—*soul*. Because these two concepts are foundational to what I will be developing in the rest of the book, it is important that I clarify what I mean by these terms.

The soul that interests me in these pages is not the technical concept of the theologian or philosopher. My use of the term is more metaphorical. I use it to refer to persons in their depths and totality, with particular emphasis on their inner life.

This, it seems to me, is comparable to Jesus' use of the term. For example, when he spoke of his soul's being crushed with sorrow (Matthew 26:38), he was speaking of his inner world of feelings and hope. The same is true when he promised rest for the souls of those who come to him (Matthew 11:29). The soul rest that Jesus offers touches the whole of our being—physical, spiritual and psychological—but is particularly focused on our inner self.

A soul friendship is therefore a relationship to which I bring my whole self, especially my inner self. And the care that I offer for the other person in a soul friendship is a care for his or her whole self, especially the inner self. Soul friends seek to safeguard each other's uniqueness and nurture the growth of each other's inner self. They seek to meet each other as whole people and help each other become whole people. They offer each other the sacred gift of accompaniment on the human journey.

What, then, does the concept of spirituality add to this? I use the term *spirituality* to refer to a person's awareness of and response to the Divine. On the basis of this I would argue that to be human is to be spiritual. Everybody has some awareness of God. We differ only in the degree of that awareness and the nature of the response we make to it. We all face the inescapable challenge of working out our existence in relationship to God. That is our spirituality. That is what it means to be human.

Christian spirituality is, of course, something much more specific. Christian spirituality involves *working out our existence* within the context of the Christian faith and community. More precisely, it is the deep relationship with God that exists when the human spirit is grounded in God's Spirit. Spirituality is not Christian if it is not centered in the Spirit. Christian spirituality is our response to the Spirit. He is the one who initiates and guides the journey for Christians.

For Christians, the spiritual journey is at the core of the human journey. We believe that the ultimate fulfillment of our humanity is found in union with God through Christ. Nothing is therefore more important than discovering and actualizing the unique self-in-Christ that is my eternal destiny. This is the core of Christian spirituality.

Spiritual friends. If you are making significant progress on the transformational journey of Christian spirituality, you have one or more friendships that support that journey. If you do not, you are not. It is that simple.

Spiritual friends nurture the development of each other's soul. Their love for each other translates into a desire that the other settle for nothing less than becoming all that he or she was intended to be. What they offer each other in response to this desire is not a professional role. Nor is it specialized expertise. Rather, it is the gift of themselves and their companionship on the transformational journey of Christian spirituality.

Spiritual friends are soul friends. This means that they care for each other as whole people, not simply as spiritual beings. Soul friends become spiritual friends when they seek to help each other attend and respond to God. In what follows I will generally refer to *spiritual friends.* I will, however, use the term *soul friends* when I wish to emphasize the basic aspects of caring for others in their depths and totality, and *true friends* when I wish to emphasize the ideal nature of these relationships.

The potential for spiritual friendship lies undetected all around us—not just in our churches but also in our homes, workplaces and communities. Tragically, those who seek such friendships often fail to see the possibilities that already exist in their lives. They fail to see a spouse as a potential soul mate, instead seeing only a husband or wife or a partner in parenting. They miss the possibility of genuinely spiritual friendships with their children, understanding their role in terms of supervision and training, not accompaniment. Other people are judged ineligible because they do not seem to be like them.

Friends, spouses and family members all have opportunities to offer each other genuine companionship on the spiritual journey. While these forms of soul friendship differ in a number of ways from the more formal and structured relationship of spiritual direction, we shall see that they also share many qualities. Ideally, they also form the dynamic core of the church. Spiritual communities are, after all, simply networks of spiritual friendships.

Spiritual direction. The second form of soul friendship that we shall examine is spiritual direction. Spiritual direction is more structured and less mutual than spiritual friendship.

Often referred to by such terms as *mentoring, discipleship* or *spiritual guidance* (these all describing slightly different but closely related forms of relationship), spiritual direction has been recently discovered by large numbers of Protestants. But it is more appropriate to describe this rise of interest as a rediscovery than as a discovery. Spiritual direction is an ancient form of Christian soul care that goes back to the earliest days of the church. It has never really gone away. It is just that large sectors of the Christian church have forgotten their own heritage.

In its classical form, spiritual direction is a one-on-one relationship organized around prayer and conversation directed toward deepening intimacy with God. As we shall see, spiritual directors are not experts, nor do they direct. They do not follow a standardized curriculum or implement a prepackaged program. Rather, they journey with others who, like themselves, are committed to the process of spiritual transformation in Christ. And most important, they seek to help those with whom they journey discern the presence and leading of the Spirit of God—the One Jesus sent as our true Spiritual Director.

Sacred companions. To describe spiritual directors and friends as "sacred companions" is to note the way they help us become more aware of the presence of the sacred. The supreme gift that anyone can give another is to help that person live life more aware of the presence of God. Sacred companions help us remember that this is our Father's world. They help us hear his voice, be aware of his presence and see his footprints as we walk through life. They accompany us on a journey that is made sacred not by their presence but by the presence of God. In doing so, they make the journey sacred. In doing so, they help us live with a keener awareness of the sacred.

Speaking Personally

Before embarking on an exploration of these forms of spiritual companionship, I would like to say a word about how I, a clinical psychologist, happen to be writing a book on spiritual direction and friendship.

While I have long been interested in the interaction of the psychological and spiritual dimensions of the soul, until recently the focus of my work and writing has been more psychological than spiritual. Most of my previous books were on counseling or psychotherapy. While they all focus on spiritual considerations as important dimensions of such clinical activities, they are primarily addressed to professionals.

I am in no way turning my back on counseling or my professional discipline of clinical psychology. I remain deeply impressed by the value of psychology, not simply as a technology of change but as an aid to understanding the dynamics of the soul. I also remain deeply committed to training counselors and psychotherapists and to providing therapeutic services myself.

However, I am concerned about the predominantly therapeutic face of soul care in our culture's church and society. We have entrusted the care of the inner life of persons to experts who understand their role primarily in problem-solving and therapeutic terms. But therapeutic soul care should not be the model of Christian soul care. Nor should clinically trained professionals be relied on to provide the bulk of such care.

While counselors and therapists have an important role to play in restoring wholeness that has been lost, spiritual friends and directors have an equally important role in helping others become all they were intended to be. It is my hope that the predominantly therapeutic face of contemporary Christian soul care will be balanced by an increasingly spiritual one as more Christians offer themselves in relationships of sacred companionship. The care of souls is much too important to be left to clinical professionals.

The Passions of an Amateur

I write about spiritual friendship and direction as an amateur, not as a professional. I hold no formal credentials in these areas, nor do I make any pretense of expertise.

What I know about spiritual friendship and direction comes first and foremost from the experience of journeying with my own spiritual friends. I have also been richly blessed by my exposure to spiritual direction through several personal experiences of receiving it, through reading and a modest amount of training, and by a number of years of offering it to others. These experiences have not made me an expert. They have, however, fueled my passion for spiritual companionship. It is on that basis that I write this book. Amateurs do what they do out of passion. This precisely describes my feelings about the enormous value of the gift of spiritual friendship and direction.

In recent years the church has been tragically marginalized as a provider of soul care. The rise of the therapeutic culture dominating the West in the last century led to an artificial separation of the psychological and spiritual aspects of persons. The acceptance of this distinction resulted in the church's being judged relevant to only the spiritual part of persons. I feel very concerned about this development and have committed two decades of work to reversing it.

If the church is to be restored to its rightful place of relevance to and preeminence in supporting the care and cure of souls, we must equip and encourage people to offer themselves to others in relationships of soul friendship and spiritual companionship. This will continue to include counselors. And it will require many more well-trained spiritual directors. But it will also require parents, spouses and friends who refuse to settle for anything less than the genuine spiritual friendships for which they themselves long. It also needs elders, small group leaders and others who understand how to structure relationships in ways that best nurture spiritual growth. My commitment to assist in these efforts has been the motivation for this book.

I offer this book with the prayer that it may be used by God to raise up an army of people ready to accompany others on the spiritual journey. In other words, I want it to make a difference. To that end, I have included questions for reflection and discussion at the end of each chapter. Simply reading a book is often insufficient to produce changes in behavior. Prayerful reflection and discussion with others always help unpack the implications of what we read and prepare for any changes that the Spirit may suggest. It is my hope, then, that these opportunities for reflection will be useful to individuals and groups who read what follows.

First Sunday of Lent, 2001
Kuala Lumpur, Malaysia

Acknowledgments

This book is the product of the companionship of a number of special people in my life. I wish to thank them for their many gifts to me, gifts that have made this book possible.

First and foremost, I again thank my wife and closest friend, Juliet, for her accompaniment on the incredible adventure that we have shared for three decades. The understandings of the spiritual journey presented in these pages have all been learned with her, many through her.

I also express deep gratitude to Larry Crabb, whose support and encouragement in the writing of this book were extravagant and humbling. I am honored to have him provide the foreword and thankful for the gift of his friendship. I also thank my good friend Gary Moon for his helpful suggestions. The book would have been better had I been able to implement more of them. But more important, I am the better for his friendship.

David and Bonnie Sigston, Simon Yiu-Chen Lee, Zoila Carandang, and Ed and Eileen Plantinga also read the manuscript and offered helpful suggestions and encouragement. I thank them for their companionship and support. I also thank Fred Gingerich and Sonia Martinez for the opportunity to present some of this material at a seminar and retreat in Manila. Feedback from these groups was most helpful in the final revisions of the manuscript that were under way during those days.

Paul Groen I thank for the conversation that led to the inclusion of a chapter on spiritual accompaniment groups. His challenge to find a way to make spiritual direction more available was much appreciated, as his friendship has been over many years.

I also wish to thank Bob Fryling and his wonderful team at Inter-Varsity Press for the welcome they have given me. I particularly thank Al Hsu for his exceptionally fine editorial work and the anonymous reviewers he recruited whose feedback was so helpful.

Finally, I wish to acknowledge the many people who have journeyed with me in retreats, spiritual direction and psychotherapy. You may have thought of me accompanying you but not realized how much your lives have touched mine. Believe me when I say that they have. It was in those journeys that we shared that I discovered much of what I now share with others.

Part One

SPIRITUAL FRIENDSHIP

1

The Transformational Journey

I have always enjoyed travel. Intellectually and spiritually I have also always been on a quest—always restless and always seeking. While recently reading a book about spiritual styles,[1] I was struck to see that it described people within the contemplative style (which fits me pretty well) as on an endless spiritual pilgrimage. It also described me exactly when it identified the attraction of such people to the image of the journey as a metaphor for life. Perhaps it is not surprising, then, that I frame this book on spiritual friendship in terms of accompaniment on a journey.

However, to describe spirituality in terms of a journey is to employ a metaphor that connects us solidly with the biblical account of the nature of Christian faith. Both Old and New Testaments frequently present faith as a response to a call to a journey—a journey of following and trusting God as he leads us on the

---

[1]Corinne Ware, *Discover Your Spiritual Type* (Bethesda, Md.: Alban Institute, 1995).

adventure he has planned for us.

Consider, for example, Abraham. God asked Abraham to leave his country and his relatives and go to a land that he would subsequently be shown. Logically this made no sense. People with families and responsibilities do not generally set forth into an unknown wilderness on the prompting of their God, particularly without knowing where they are heading. But Abraham did exactly that. He agreed to follow his God on a journey that would leave him and the world forever changed.

And remember the journey of the children of Israel as they followed God out of Egypt and into the wilderness. Tracing their route throughout the forty years of wandering in what is now Saudi Arabia would suggest that they were lost. But they were precisely where they were supposed to be—following God around the wilderness until they underwent the desired character transformation. They thought their call was simply a deliverance from Egypt to the Promised Land of milk and honey. But while God did indeed have in mind their deliverance, his plan was for deliverance from much more than the Egyptians. God had in mind their deliverance from themselves. They were called to a journey of transformation, not simply to another country in which to live.

Finally, also remember the call Jesus issued to his disciples. To Simon and Andrew it was simply "Follow me and I will make you fish for people" (Mark 1:17 NRSV). To Levi it was an even terser "Follow me" (Mark 2:14). Again the call was to a journey, not to a destination. And again it was a call to a journey that would leave them forever changed.

The essence of Christian spirituality is following Christ on a journey of personal transformation. The distant land to which we are called is not heaven. Nor is it some external, physical place. The distant land is the new creature into which Christ wishes to fashion us—the whole and holy person that finds his or her uniqueness, identity and calling in Christ. Spiritual friends accompany each other on that journey.

The soul's journey in Christian spirituality is a journey of becoming, not simply of doing or even being. This is why it gives priority to the inner self. The transformation that occurs in Christian spirituality moves from the inside out. This is the significance of Christ's constant emphasis on the heart.

Changes in our behavior are important, but our motives for what we do are even more important. Recall how Jesus structures the Sermon on the Mount with the formula "You have heard how it was said . . . but I say this to you" (see Matthew 5—7). What is the higher standard that is set by Christ? It is the state of the heart. Motives count. Private thoughts count. The inner self counts and in fact is the primary focus of the personal transformation that Jesus calls conversion.

The Route for the Journey

As with the journey Abraham was asked to undertake, it is impossible to specify precisely the route that has to be followed in a soul's journey of transformation. This is because rather than following a map, in this journey we follow a person—Jesus. Jesus does not tell us where to go; he simply asks us to follow him.

The Christian spiritual journey requires us to overcome the temptation to follow other people rather than Jesus himself. If we are blessed, we will have experiences of seeing him in spiritual friends or other Christians who share our journey. In these circumstances it is sometimes tempting to think that following them is following Jesus. But it is not. Spiritual friends help us most when they make clear that their job is to point the way, not to lead the way. And the Way to which they should point is Jesus.

An equally important temptation for those seeking to offer spiritual friendship is to assume that one's own route is best for others. How easy it is to think that everyone should meet God in the way and places that I do. How easily I imagine that everyone should follow the same path of prayer, devotion or service as I have followed.

The task of spiritual friends is to help us discern the presence, will and leading of the Spirit of God. Spiritual friends provide a seri-

ous disservice when they authoritatively dictate the specific path
we should follow. In so doing they seek to give us a map of their own
creation. At best, this will distract us from a focus on Jesus and his
Spirit. At worst, it leads us to focus on a map rather than God himself—and that is the sin of idolatry.

However, while we may not be able to describe the route in
detail, we can certainly say some things about it. Following John
Calvin, Protestants have generally sketched three broad stages of
the journey—conversion, sanctification and glorification. *Conversion* refers to the initiation of our new life in Christ, *sanctification*
to growth in holiness and *glorification* to the completion of this
process when we receive a new resurrection body.

Because only the first two stages involve this life, Protestants
have had the most to say about this part of the journey. After pointing people to conversion as the beginning of the journey and
encouraging them in the basic spiritual disciplines (prayer, Bible
study, church involvement and so on), Protestants have often run
short of specific advice as to the route for the journey. This leads
directly to the major difference between what is commonly called
discipling (or mentoring) and spiritual direction. Discipling, as it is
generally practiced, focuses on the first steps for those either new
in following Christ or those who have not yet progressed very far on
the journey. Spiritual direction focuses more on later stages of the
journey and is usually judged most relevant to those who seek to
deepen an already-present practice of prayer.

The formulation of the journey adopted by Roman Catholic and
Eastern Orthodox Christians has also included three stages—purgation, illumination and union. *Purgation* refers to the purification of
one's character through confession of sin and adoption of an attitude of
detachment from worldly possessions and values. *Illumination* refers
to a growing personal experience of God's love and peace and an
increasing willingness to surrender one's will to God. *Union* has to do
with an overall harmony between one's being and God himself, focusing particularly on surrender to his will as his Spirit becomes ours.

Practical mysticism. Some of the most helpful discussion of the more advanced stages of Christian spiritual transformation comes from Christian mystics, both Catholic and Protestant. Mystics commit themselves to the pursuit of a personal, experiential knowing of God, particularly the experience of union with God. What they have to tell us about the spiritual journey is of great potential help to anyone who seriously seeks to know God more deeply or help others to do the same. Here I mention just two such authors, one Protestant and one Roman Catholic. Others are introduced in the "Suggestions for Further Reading" at the end of the book.

In her book *Interior Castle,* Teresa of Ávila (1515-1582) portrays the spiritual journey as movement through a series of seven rooms of a castle. Progress on the journey is movement toward the innermost room, where Christ dwells and where we encounter him most directly. What Teresa describes by means of this metaphor is the deepening life of prayer. Movement through the rooms of the castle involves progression from vocal prayer to meditation to contemplation and finally union with God. The deepening intimacy with God that she describes is achieved through love, not simply knowledge. This knowing of God is a knowing of the heart, not simply a knowing of the head. It is falling in love with the Lord.

Evelyn Underhill (1875-1941) also portrays the spiritual journey in terms of a progression in prayer. In *Practical Mysticism* she suggests that preparation for any serious progress in prayer demands three things: (1) the discipline of our attention, (2) a simplification of our lifestyle and (3) a reorientation of our affections and our will. The approach to prayer that she teaches begins with what she calls recollection, progresses to meditation and then proceeds to contemplation. This progression involves first acquiring the discipline of concentration and then allowing it to be replaced with the surrender to God's Spirit that is involved in contemplation. In contemplation we experience God directly rather than merely thinking about him. Referring to this as an experience of sensation without thought, Underhill is describing what Teresa and others call union with God.

These two women's descriptions of the terrain crossed in the spiritual journey are similar. Along with St. John of the Cross, Thomas Merton, St. Francis of Sales and numerous other Christian mystics, they emphasize the importance of prayer on this journey. Progression in the school of prayer is understood as involving not simply discipline but also movement from prayer of the head (verbal prayer) to prayer of the heart (prayer of loving attunement to God's presence). Although such prayer should never be expected to replace worded prayers, it will deepen them. It also holds the possibility of helping us make significant progress toward the goal of praying without ceasing.

Embracing mystery. Protestants are often suspicious of mysticism. Sometimes associating it with magic or occultism, they may assume that *Christian mysticism* is an oxymoron. This is a serious misunderstanding. The Christian mystics offer tremendously rich resources for those seeking to deepen their life of prayer and intimacy with God. That help is both most needed and yet most often resisted by those predisposed by background or personality to be overly intellectual in their life and faith.

This was certainly my experience. For many years my knowing of God was primarily a matter of knowing *about* him. Faith was more intellectual assent than emotional reliance or trust, and I related to God much more with my head than my heart. Despite the fact that the Word was made flesh, I tended to turn him back into words—my preferred medium of engagement. This left me feeling smugly dismissive of experiential approaches to Christian spirituality that are based on what I judged to be theologically weak foundations. Not surprisingly, it also resulted in a personal experience of God that was tremendously arid.

The extent of my spiritual impoverishment first became obvious in my mid-thirties. I began to feel dissatisfied with my limited direct experience of God's presence. I was spiritually restless and filled with longing. I envied those who seemed to love God, not just their ideas about him. I longed to know him personally and experientially, not just know about him.

My spiritual hunger led me to read the classics of Christian spirituality—the authors I have just named among them. I had many of these books on my shelf, but I had just dabbled in them, never expecting their way to be mine. Now I devoured them. Read hand in hand with my Bible, they helped me encounter the Word behind the words of Scripture. They also helped me take first steps toward meeting God not just in my head but also in my heart.

I felt as if I was being reborn. It was a spiritual birthing, comparable in spiritual impact to my conversion of two decades earlier. God gave me the Christian mystics as spiritual friends and used them to direct me toward a deeper experience of him. I am still far from the depth of encounter with God for which I long. But I am closer than I was.

From distant places and times these wise Christians are able to reach across generations, cultures and denominational boundaries to offer soul-nourishing guidance to those seeking accompaniment on the Christian spiritual journey. We should be careful not to neglect or despise them simply because they may seem unlike us— possibly overly serious, perhaps too otherworldly, maybe associated with another branch of the Christian church. In reality they are fellow pilgrims who, as part of the cloud of witnesses that surrounds us on the journey, offer us important accompaniment and spiritual guidance.

Mystery will always be enigmatic. But it need not be feared. A spiritual journey that seeks to eliminate all that is mysterious will never take us far enough from our comfort zone for genuine transformation.

The Destination of the Journey

I have been speaking of maps of the terrain covered in the Christian spiritual journey. But what can be said about the journey's destination? Any journey must have an objective, and any process of transformation must have a goal. How, then, can we describe the goal of the Christian journey of spiritual transformation?

The intended destination of the Christian journey has been described in a variety of ways. Often it is depicted in terms of becoming Christlike, acquiring the fruit of the Spirit or becoming holy. The Westminster Confession describes it as coming to know God and enjoying him forever. Eastern Orthodox Christians have frequently spoken of moving from imaging God to resembling him (thus emphasizing what Western Protestants have described as sanctification). Roman Catholics have typically spoken of the goal of the journey as union with God. Each of these captures important interrelated dimensions of the personal transformation that is part of being a Christ follower. They can, I think, be summarized by three closely interrelated master goals of the journey: (1) becoming a great lover, (2) becoming whole and holy, and (3) becoming our true self-in-Christ.

Becoming a Great Lover

No account of Christian spirituality is complete if it fails to give a central place to love. God is love. He has poured this love into our hearts through the Holy Spirit (Romans 5:5). Offering us his love, he desires that we become like him—great lovers.

John Wesley described sanctification as the process of renewal in the image of Christ. Central to what this meant for Wesley was loving as Christ did. And how did Christ love? He loved God with all his heart, soul, mind and strength, and his neighbor as himself. Christian spiritual transformation is, in the language of the Wesleyans, being made perfect in love—Christ's love becoming our love.

The ordering of the commands in Christ's summary of the law is important. Love begins with God. Hence our transformation into great lovers begins not by loving ourselves more deeply, nor even by loving our neighbor more purely, but by falling head over heels in love with God.

How do we learn to love God? The answer is by coming to know him. But the knowing that leads to love can never be simply a head knowing—a knowing about God. The knowing that leads to devotion must be based on a heart knowing. To really know God we must know his love experientially. I begin to love God when I know—not simply believe—that God loves me. When the thing about me that I most deeply know is that I am deeply loved by God, I have taken the first step toward a heart knowing of God. I have also taken the first step toward becoming genuinely loving of others.

The Practice of the Presence of God presents Brother Lawrence's simple secret of prayer that he learned while washing dishes in a monastery kitchen for a significant percentage of the seventeenth century. His "secret" is alarmingly simple; it entails a loving turning of his eyes toward God at all times. Brother Lawrence's prayer method is in fact nothing more than a discipline for the cultivation of a love relationship. How does one come to love another but by paying loving attention to that person?

To know God we must think *of* him, not simply *about* him. We must learn to become attentive to his presence with us. We must learn to spend time gazing on him, being still before him and focused on him. And we must learn to listen to him. These disciplines of loving attention form the basis of the development of a love relationship with God.

Genuine love of God spills over into *neighbor love*. Jesus tells us that our love of others is to be the sign to the world that we are his followers (John 13:35). John tells us that everyone who loves is born of God and knows God, and everyone who does not love others does not know God (1 John 4:7-8). The relationship between knowing God and love could not be much clearer.

The demands of love. Writing these words makes me painfully aware of how short of these ideals I fall. I recall how harsh I recently was with a very dear friend, letting my irritation over an extremely petty matter spill out in a totally inappropriate and hurtful comment. Then, after asking his forgiveness and praying fervently for the ability to love my friend just as he is, I did the same thing again just a few weeks later.

How I wish God had set something—anything—other than love as the supreme measure of spiritual progress. Recognizing the impoverishment of my love of both God and others is so discouraging. It's the most depressing thing I have encountered in my Christ following.

My first response to the limitations of my love is always the same—to try harder. I pray for love with more fervor. And I try to love with more diligence. But nothing seems to change. Then I recall that once again I have got it all backwards. God doesn't want me to try to become more loving. He wants me to absorb his love so that it flows out from me.

And so I return again to knowing myself as deeply loved by God. I meditate on his love, allowing my focus to be on him and his love for me, not me and my love for him. And slowly things begin to change. My heart slowly begins to warm and soften. I begin to experience new levels of love for God. And slowly, almost imperceptibly, I begin to see others through God's eyes of love. I begin to experience God's love for others.

Only love is capable of genuine transformation. Willpower is inadequate. Even spiritual effort is not up to the task. If we are to become great lovers, we must return again and again to the great love of the Great Lover. Thomas Merton reminds us that the root of Christian love is not the will to love but the faith to believe that one is deeply loved by God. Returning to that great love—a love that was there for us before we experienced any rejection and that will be there for us after all other rejections take place—is our true spiritual work.

Embarking on the journey of Christian spiritual transformation is enrolling in the divine school of love. Our primary assignment in this school is not so much study and practice as letting ourselves be deeply loved by our Lord.

Becoming Whole and Holy

The reason I like to describe the goal of the Christian spiritual journey as becoming both whole and holy is that it reminds us that the focus of God's love and salvation is not some part of us but our whole person. Jesus does not love some immaterial or eternal part of me. He loves *me*. And Jesus did not die so that some part of me would be saved; he died so that in my whole being I would be made anew. Anything less than this trivializes salvation and fractures human personhood in ways God never intended.

Too often the Christian journey is understood simply in terms of becoming like God. While this is an essential component, if we only emphasize this aspect of it, we are likely to develop a spirituality that deemphasizes our humanity. The goal of the Christian spiritual journey is not to become less human and more divine; it is to become more fully human. Salvation is not to rescue us from our humanity; it is to redeem our humanity.

Tragically, some visions of the Christian spiritual journey have led people to deny entire aspects of their humanity. Some people have rejected their sexuality, others their intellect, emotions or playfulness. All who do so limp along the path to wholeness and holiness. But rather than bring their lameness to God for healing, they tend to wear it as a badge of spiritual honor.

Spirituality not grounded in humanness is no earthly good. Worse, it can actually be dangerous. Spirituality that apparently makes us more like God but fails to make us more genuinely human actually destroys our personhood. If embracing humanness was good enough for Jesus, how can we despise it? To become like Jesus and take on his character, we must—like him—embrace our humanity and work out our spirituality within it. The authentic journey of Christian spirituality must always involve redemption of our humanity, never its denial or attempted crucifixion.

This draws our attention to the importance and interdependence of knowing both God and self. As argued by John Calvin in the opening pages of his *Institutes of the Christian Religion*, there is no deep knowing of God apart from a deep knowing of self and no deep knowing of self apart from a deep knowing of God. Meister Eckhart, the fourteenth-century Christian mystic and theologian, said the same thing two centuries earlier. Knowing God and knowing self are both necessary for wholeness and holiness.

How tragic it is when a person invests all his or her energy in knowing God and none in genuinely knowing him or herself. And how terrifying when such a person is in a position of leadership or influence. Christian maturity demands that we know God and ourselves, recognizing that deep knowing of each supports deeper knowing of the other.

While holiness emphasizes taking on the character of God, wholeness reminds us that doing so does not make us gods or even angels—it makes us more completely human. St. Irenaeus reminds us that the glory of God is a fully alive human being. God is in the business of making us fully human and fully alive. This is the abundant life promised by Jesus (John 10:10). Our vitality, our genuine fullness of life, points back to God, the author of life. In so doing it gives God glory.

The purpose of salvation is to make whole that which is broken. The Christian spiritual journey settles for nothing less than such wholeness. But genuine wholeness cannot occur apart from holiness. In *The Holiness of God* R. C. Sproul notes that the pattern of God's transforming encounters with humans is always the same. God appears; humans respond with fear because of their sin; God forgives our sins and heals us (holiness and wholeness); God then sends us out to serve him. This means that holiness and wholeness are the interrelated goals of the Christian spiritual journey. Holiness is the goal of the spiritual journey because God is holy and commands that we be holy (Leviticus 11:44).

Holiness involves taking on the life and character of a holy God by means of a restored relationship to him. This relationship heals our most fundamental disease—our separation from our Source, our Redeemer, the Great Lover of our soul. This relationship is therefore simultaneously the source of our holiness and of our wholeness.

Human beings were designed for intimate relationship with God and cannot find fulfillment of their true and deepest self apart from that relationship. Holiness does not involve the annihilation of our identity with a simple transplant of God's identity. Rather, it involves the transformation of our self, made possible by the work of God's Spirit within us. Holiness is becoming like the God with whom we live in intimate relationship. It is acquiring his Spirit and allowing spirit to be transformed by Spirit. It is finding and living our life in Christ, and then discovering that Christ's life and Spirit are our life and spirit. This is the journey of Christian spiritual transformation. This is the process of becoming whole and holy.

Becoming Our True Self-in-Christ

The mystical teaching of the New Testament about the relationship between our life and Christ's life within us has frequently been misunderstood, often with serious consequences. Failure to understand this matter has led to dangerous and misleading teaching about the self. It has also sometimes led people to attempt to crucify the wrong thing.

Paul speaks of being crucified with Christ but of Christ's living in him (Galatians 2:20). But which part of us is to be crucified and which is to be alive in Christ? What is the relationship between my self and Christ who lives in me? After all, Christ is described as living in me; so there must be some "me" that survives the crucifixion. What, then, does this tell us about the goal of the Christian transformational journey?

The notion of becoming our true self-in-Christ emphasizes the fact that there are true and false ways of living. Most of us can identify ways we wear masks of our own creation. The fact that we are capable of thinking about how we want to behave in any given situation shows that we can make choices about this. Inherent in this choice is the fact that we can choose to live a lie; we can choose to pretend to be someone or something that we are not.

In his very helpful discussion of the true and false self, Basil Pennington suggests that my false self is made up of what I have, what I do and what people think of me. It is constructed, therefore, out of false attachments.[2]

Stop for a moment and think about how you introduce yourself. It will tell you a lot about how you want others to see you. Whenever I invite people to see me in terms of what I have or do, I am living out of my false self.

Pennington suggests that Christ's temptations in the wilderness were temptations to live out of such a false center. First the tempter invited him to turn stones into bread. But Jesus said no to the invitation to establish himself on the basis of his doing. Then the tempter invited him to throw himself from the top of the temple into the crowds below, so they would immediately recognize him as the Messiah. Again Jesus rejected the temptation. He chose not to base his identity on the acclaim of others. Finally the tempter offered him all the kingdoms of the world. But once again Jesus rejected the offer, refusing to find his identity in possessions or power.

Jesus knew who he was before God and in God. He could therefore resist temptations to live his life out of a false center based on possessions, actions or the esteem of others.

Merton suggests that at the core of our false ways of being there is always a sinful refusal to surrender to God's will.[3] My reluctance to find my identity and fulfillment in Christ leaves me vulnerable to living out of a false center. It leaves me no alternative but to create a self of my own making.

This is where the problem begins. The self I am called from eternity to be has meaning only in relation to Christ. The unique self that I am called to be is never a self I simply dream up and decide I'd like to be. It is always and only the self that I actually

---

[2]Basil Pennington, *True Self/False Self* (New York: Crossroad, 2000).
[3]Thomas Merton, *New Seeds of Contemplation* (New York: New Directions, 1961).

am in Christ. This is my eternal self. This is the self I am intended to be. This is the only self that will allow me to be truly whole and holy.

What, then, should be crucified? Call it my sinful self or my false selves; what need to be crucified are my ways of living apart from surrender to God's will. It is not radical enough to try to stop committing sin. This is too superficial. Ignatius of Loyola suggests that sin is ultimately a refusal to believe that what God wants is my happiness and fulfillment. When I fail to believe this, I am tempted to sin—to take my life into my own hands, assuming that I am in the best position to determine what will lead to my happiness. As I become convinced that God wants nothing more than my fulfillment, surrender to his will is increasingly possible.

If our sinful and false ways of being are what we are to crucify, what are we to actualize? The self that I am to become is Christ in me; it is my self-in-Christ. Both say the same thing. Both point to the unique self that is found only in Christ and in the fullness of his life in and through me. This is the good news of Galatians 2:20. This is the goal of the Christian transformational journey.

Properly understood, these three intended destinations of the journey—becoming a great lover, becoming whole and holy, and becoming my true self-in-Christ—demonstrate just how radical Christian spiritual transformation really is. At times these goals seem absolutely unattainable, impossibly far from where I am at the moment. Authentic transformation seems so tiresome, so long a reach. I simply want to stay where I am. I want to stop the journey and make my destination wherever I presently find myself.

If I were making the spiritual journey on my own, I suspect that I would do just that. But I do not need to make it on my own. In fact I dare not.

Journeying Together

A friend who was unhappy with the church had an interesting reply when I recently asked him why he continued to attend, even if intermittently. He answered that he was afraid that he would stop growing if he dropped out of church. He went on: "Even if I get nothing out of the sermon and even if I have trouble encountering God in the rest of the service, church keeps me in touch with others on the spiritual journey. Spiritual growth is just too hard to maintain alone."

He was right. Christian spirituality demands journeying together. This means more than the accompaniment of the Spirit of God. It also includes the accompaniment of fellow pilgrims.

Contemporary discussions of the soul often place the emphasis of care on one's own soul. While this is important, the emphasis in Christian soul care is always on the care of the souls of others. The care of souls is an act of neighbor love. When Jesus taught that we should love our neighbor as ourselves, he was making a point about care of others, not self-care. The principle of self-care is implicit within it but is not its essence. Careful attention to one's inner life is an indispensable prerequisite of caring for the souls of others. But when we make soul care primarily self-care, we trivialize a concept that lies at the core of the mission of the Christian church.

The Christian spiritual journey is a journey we take with others. Each of us must take our own journey, and for each of us that journey will be unique. But none of us is intended to make that journey alone. The myth of the solitary Christian making his or her way alone to paradise flies in the face of everything the Bible teaches about the church as the body of Christ (1 Corinthians 12:12-31). We are parts of one body as we follow Christ on the journey of personal transformation. We cannot make the journey apart from spiritual companions and community.

I am the sort of person whose spirit readily responds to the challenge of great adventures. Setting off into the wilderness without a clear destination appeals to something deep within me. Long-distance, single-handed sailing appeals to the same part of me. But people like me who delight in great adventures are often rugged individualists who prefer to pursue their adventure alone. The Christian spiritual journey does not work this way. It is not like running a marathon. No one can make any real progress on this journey alone. Journeying together is the only way to effect the personal transformation that is the goal of the adventure.

We need companions on the Christian journey for a number of reasons. First among these is that the deep knowing of both self and God foundational to Christian spirituality demands deep knowing of and being known by others. Neither knowing God nor knowing self can progress very far apart from others who are able and willing to offer us help. Some spiritual friends offer us help in knowing ourselves, while others offer help in knowing God. The best offer us both. This is a central feature of the gift of a true spiritual friend.

Note that I said that deep knowing of self and God requires deep knowing of and by others. Intimate relationships with others prepare us for intimacy with God. It is hard for me to imagine how someone could experience an intimate personal relationship with God and be unable to experience such a relationship with others. The gift of those who accompany us on the spiritual journey is not merely that they help us know God and ourselves. It is also that, by virtue of their relationship to us, they help us become people who are capable of intimacy—an essential element in the Christian character that is the goal of the journey.

Love is cultivated only in close soul relationships. We can probably learn something about love in interactions with strangers, but the transforming work of becoming the great lovers that Christ desires us to be demands the grist of more intimate relationships. It is in soul friendships that we encounter the greatest possibilities for progress in the school of love. Journeying together brings opportunities for discovering the magnitude of our narcissism and developing a heart of genuine love.

Reflecting on the Transformational Journey
Before progressing further on our journey together, let us take a

moment to review the terrain we have already covered. To help make this reflection practical, I also offer some questions for personal or group discussion, as well as one or two suggestions.

Although I have described Christian spirituality as a journey, not everyone thinks of it in these terms. Perhaps you have tended to view it primarily as a commitment or even a set of obligations. Or possibly you have understood it as an identity.

In its most basic terms Christian spirituality is a relationship with God. Perhaps the most remarkable thing to notice about this Christian God is that is it he who has sought us out, not we him. In fact, anything that we experience as desire for him is simply the result of his Spirit's calling us to himself. Spirituality is the response of spirit to Spirit.

- Reflect on your own journey to this point. What were your earliest spiritual stirrings? How has God tended to call you to growth and to himself over the course of your journey? What difference does it make to understand your journey as the response of spirit to Spirit?
- If you are not already doing so, consider beginning a journal as a place for prayerful, regular reflection on your spiritual journey. Use your journal as a place to dialogue with God about the questions at the end of each chapter.

Christian spirituality is about becoming all we were meant to be. In this chapter I have described this as becoming great lovers who are whole and holy because we have begun to discover our true self-in-Christ. It is also about becoming truly and fully human and truly and fully ourselves. It is life's greatest possible adventure!

- How do you understand the goal of Christian spirituality? What do you consider to be the major markers of progress on the journey? How do you assess your own progress on the journey?
- How do you respond to the possibility of a personal, experiential knowing of God? If you find yourself with much more head than heart knowing of God, what makes it difficult to experience the intimacy with God that Teresa of Ávila describes as a "knowing

through love"? Is this something you would like to experience more fully? Journal on your desire and fears, and then seek an opportunity to discuss this with someone you think may have greater heart knowledge of God.

One important feature of the call to the Christian spiritual journey is that it is a call to follow Jesus, not simply to go somewhere or do something. Christ's call to us is never just a call to conversion. This call is equally relevant at every stage of the spiritual journey.

❊ Read several of the Gospel accounts of Christ's call to his disciples to follow him, and place yourself in the story as the one to whom Jesus is speaking (Mark 1:14-19; 2:13-17; Luke 5:1-11, 27-32; John 1:35-51). What is Jesus saying to you today?

No one is called to make this spiritual journey alone. Of course we are never really alone, because we have the companionship of the Spirit as we seek to follow Jesus. But we also need human companions—both spiritual friends and spiritual directors. These are the people, we shall see, who accompany us on this transformational journey. They do so not simply to help us grow but because they love us and want to share our lives. In doing so they offer us significant opportunities for spiritual growth—opportunities we will examine in the chapters that follow.

❊ Is there someone with whom you could share aspects of your spiritual journey that to this point you have not? Consider doing so as a way of finding new and more meaningful ways of journeying with others. Pray that God might help you identify a person with whom you can discuss some of your reflections on this chapter.

2

Hospitality, Presence & Dialogue

One of the great privileges of being a parent is the opportunity to learn from your children. I recently learned something important from my son about being a companion on a journey.

Sean works as a tour leader in Central and South America, leading small groups of people on adventures that keep participants physically active and close to local culture. On a typical six-week tour he might lead a group of five to eight people through a half-dozen countries—exploring the jungle, climbing mountains, experiencing local food and customs, and all the time working hard to keep everyone in his group happy. He excels at what he does and loves his job—it is perfect for someone like him, in his twenties, living life on the edge and on the move.

In a recent e-mail he asked me what I was writing at the moment. As I described this book, I realized it was a great opportunity to get some help in thinking about the role of a companion on a journey. So I asked Sean to describe what is involved in being a successful tour leader.

"That's simple," he wrote back. "All it takes is liking people enough that you don't mind being with them eighteen hours a day, listening to them enough to know what they want and like even better than they do, and being ready to be their mother and take care of whatever goes wrong!"

Being an adventure tour leader and a companion on the spiritual journey are not exactly the same. However, they share some important features. In both cases what the person does is secondary in importance to who he or she is. Being must precede doing.

Spiritual friendship is not primarily a matter of doing certain things. Often, in fact, it is precisely the opposite of doing; it is a gift of not doing—not interrupting, not attempting to solve problems, not prematurely or inappropriately advising, not assuming that what has worked for us will work for others. Stated positively: spiritual friendship is a gift of hospitality, presence and dialogue. While all of these have a component of doing—that is, they have to be lived out—they are grounded in ways of being.

The Gift of Hospitality

In *Holy Listening: The Art of Spiritual Direction* Margaret Guenther describes spiritual friendship as the gift of hospitality. The image of the hospitable host fits well with the metaphor of the journey. It reminds us that soul friends show hospitality by making space in their lives for others. Making space in my life is more demanding than giving advice, money or some other form of help. But the essence of hospitality is taking another person into my space, into my life. This is also the essence of being a soul friend.

Soul hosts prepare for their gift of hospitality by cultivating a place of quiet within themselves. This is the place where they will receive others. If I have no such place within myself, I am unable to offer myself in a gift of soul hospitality. But when I have begun to be a person with a quiet, still center, I can invite others to come and rest there. It is out of this place that soul friends offer their gifts of presence, stillness, safety and love.

God is the supreme example of this sort of soul hospitality. He was our host in creation—shaping a uniquely inviting and accommodating place for us in a garden of his creation, and then joining us there to ensure that we knew we belonged. The Garden of Eden is a wonderful metaphor for divine hospitality. It provides a graphic illustration of the possibilities of intimacy that exist in meeting others in sacred places.

Remarkably, the intimacy that God offers me is not limited to him hosting me. He also longs for me to host him—to invite him into my inner garden and to meet him there. If I am to have a place of stillness at the core of my being, it will only be because I have learned to offer hospitality to the Spirit. The Spirit, then, becomes the source of my soul hospitality as I make myself available to others.

Although I often try to pull it off, I know that I cannot really be present for another person when my inner world is filled with preoccupations and distractions. This is one of the biggest challenges I face in being present for others—being still within my own soul. Stillness is the precondition of presence. I must first be still to myself if I am to be still with another. And, of course, I must learn to be still before God if I am to learn to be still in myself. Presence begins with a still place within one's self. If I have no such still inner place, I cannot really be present for others.

Can I be still enough that I can hear God's call to me to join him in my inner garden? The reason he wants to meet me there is that this is where he wants the transformation to begin. But so often, fearing meeting him or myself in my depths, I try to arrange a rendezvous with God in some safer place outside myself. And then I wonder why God does not seem to be there.

Henri Nouwen describes the nurture of inner stillness as the cultivation of solitude of the heart. Such solitude is not a state of relaxation. Nor is it simply a matter of being alone. Solitude of heart comes from attentiveness to the presence of God. It is the prayer of spirit to Spirit, a prayer of attunement, not necessarily of words. It is a response of surrender to the Spirit of Jesus, who offers us rest for our souls.

Soul hospitality is also a gift of safety. Think of feeling safe enough with another person that without weighing words or measuring thoughts you are able to pour yourself out, trusting that the other person will keep what is worth keeping and, with a breath of kindness, blow the rest away.[1] Or listen to the twelfth-century description of spiritual direction by Aelred of Rievaulx: "What happiness, what security, what joy to have . . . one to whom you can entrust all the secrets of your heart and before whom you can place all your plans."[2] Who would not desire such a place of safety and love? Who would not want such a friendship?

Soul friendship is the gift of a place where anything can be said without fear of criticism or ridicule. It is a place where masks and pretensions can be set aside. It is a place where it is safe to share deepest secrets, darkest fears, most acute sources of shame, most disturbing questions or anxieties. It is a place of grace—a place where others are accepted as they are for the sake of who they may become.

Obviously this demands confidentiality. Unless it is clear that confidences shared will be kept within the relationship, there is no real safety. Apart from a sense of safety, there is no possibility of a genuine soul friendship.

Finally, soul hospitality is a gift of love. Genuine hospitality is always motivated by love. This is what makes both the host and the act of hospitality safe. Love is the motive for the gift of presence that the soul host offers others. Other motives may lead to an appearance of genuine presence, but none provides an acceptable substitute. Only love can support the offering of self

---

[1]This image comes from a passage in George Elliot's *Middlemarch* (New York: Penguin, 1994). However, despite a careful search, I remain unable to find the passage.
[2]Aelred of Rievaulx, *Spiritual Friendship* (Kalamazoo, Mich.: Cistercian, 1977), p. 72.

that is involved in soul hospitality.

Soul friends love people. Apart from real love for real people, we will always be dealing with secret (or not so secret) impatience, judgmentalism, disgust, resentment, envy or anger. Real people require real love if we are to give a gift of genuine presence.

I cannot think of soul hospitality without recalling a remarkable visit that I was blessed to have with Paul Tournier shortly before his death. Well into his eighties and frail at the time, this much-loved Swiss physician and author of numerous books on psychology and spirituality continued to receive guests who came to see him from around the world. Arriving with thirty eager university students, I was warmly greeted by Dr. Tournier at his home in Geneva. He invited us into his backyard. There he first spoke to each of us individually, slowly asking our names, where we were from and some questions about our lives. It was astonishing. He seemed to be—and genuinely was—interested in each of us, all of us strangers to him until that moment.

But then he offered us a gift that really took our breath away. He slowly walked to a garden shed, steadied by the arm of his nurse. After several minutes he emerged with a pile of flags. Moving toward a flagpole that was in the center of his yard, he proceeded to hoist the flag of the country of birth of each of the thirty guests. As each flag was raised, he welcomed us and told us how honored he was to have us as guests in his home. This ceremony, lasting nearly half an hour, was one of the most moving acts of hospitality I have ever witnessed.

Paul Tournier was a master host. He excelled at creating space for others in his life. He did it by maintaining a quiet, still center. This stillness emanated from him. It allowed us to feel still just by being with him. It allowed him to temporarily share the special garden that was his soul, not just his backyard.

The Gift of Genuine Presence

John O'Donohue, in *Eternal Echoes,* describes presence as soul-atmosphere. The presence of each person is unique, just as the

atmosphere in each person's home is unique. Presence involves a
sharing of something of my deepest self. Though it is difficult to
define, it is easily recognized as soon as it is encountered.

What does it mean to be genuinely present to another person?
Stillness, safety and love are preconditions for this presence. But it
is possible to experience all these things and not be able to open
myself to the other person and his or her experience in the way
that is essential for soul friends. How, then, do I allow myself to be
genuinely present for another person?

Presence begins with attentiveness. This demands that I focus on
the other person and his or her experience. Although we shall see
that the other person's experience is only part of what we attend to,
we can never be genuinely present for another person unless we
start with this. This attentiveness to the other involves setting some
things aside. It usually means setting aside my own interests and
preoccupations. It also demands that I stop analyzing what I am
hearing or rehearsing how I will respond. And as I have noted, it
also involves resisting the impulse to solve problems or fix things
that appear broken.

Think how often you have been with people who appeared to be
listening, but the sound of their own thoughts all but drowned out
the presence they were attempting to offer. Perhaps it was the echo
of their rehearsing what they would next say, or possibly it was the
noise of their inner thoughts about what you were saying. But one
way or another you knew that they were not fully present.

To be present to you means that I must be prepared, temporarily,
to be absent to me. I must therefore set aside all the things I carry
with me in consciousness all day long—my planning for what
comes next, my evaluation of how I am doing and my reflection on
what is presently transpiring. These are the noises that drown out
silence. These are the distractions that keep me focused on myself
and make it impossible for me to be present to another person.

Presence is enormously difficult. I confess that I sometimes find
it easier simply to pretend to be present—to maintain appropriate

eye contact, to do more listening than talking and to minimize any appearance of wandering thoughts. It's so tempting to believe that faking presence is an acceptable alternative to offering genuine presence. But it isn't. And at some level of awareness the other person will always recognize the difference.

Genuine presence involves being genuinely myself. I can be present for another person only when I dare to be present to myself. And as noted, I can be genuinely present to myself only when I can be genuinely present to God. Presence to another person is sharing this gift of my true self-in-Christ. It is not playing a "spiritual friend" role. It is simply being fully my authentic self and then setting this self aside as I seek to create a place within myself where I can receive another person.

Being genuinely me means being genuine. This means that what I say, I mean and believe. It also means that what I show, I feel. It means not pretending. Being genuine does not mean communicating everything I feel or think. But it does mean that what I do communicate, I genuinely feel, believe and think.

It is impossible to offer genuine presence to others if I am simply an assortment of roles. Often we wear our personas like masks, each for the correct occasion. The performance is so well rehearsed that we fail to be aware that it is a performance. But it is.

Being genuinely present to another demands that I be a real person. It demands integrity of character—a correspondence between my inner world and outward appearance. While none of us accomplishes this in any final state, spiritual friends are people committed to achieving this integrity. Becoming their true self-in-Christ forms a fundamental part of their journey of Christian spirituality. Presence does not demand perfection. But it does require that I be on a transformational journey and committed to its continuation.

Sacred companions do not play a role. They are simply themselves. Because our lives are filled with professionals who play roles, it is tempting to think that soul hospitality is another of these roles. Hence we want to know what we should do to be a good spiritual friend. While there are things spiritual friends do, these are not at the core of soul hospitality. The things we do serve as a framework for the relationship. But the relationship must be one to which I bring a genuine self.

Being genuinely present to someone also means being willing to be touched by him or her. If I genuinely bring myself to a relationship, I must be prepared to be changed by it. Anything less than this means that I am not really present. Being genuinely present means that I may be affected by your feelings. I may be influenced by your beliefs. Professional neutrality seeks to minimize this sort of influence on the one offering care, making all impact unidirectional.

Power left Jesus when someone in a crowd touched the hem of his garment. Jesus was present to everyone he encountered, even when they came up from behind and surreptitiously sought to steal some of his healing power by touching his clothing. Jesus was not immune to the impact of the people he encountered. Had he been, he would have been less than an incarnation of Divine Love. But he did not come to play some role or content himself simply to communicate a divine message. Rather, accepting his calling as being the message, he met people in and through his humanity and demonstrated unparalleled presence in his encounters.

Attending to the Presence

But ultimately the presence that transforms lives is not mine but God's. As I bring my true self-in-Christ to relationships of spiritual friendship, what the other person encounters is not just me but Christ in me. Spiritual friends help each other discern God's presence and respond to him in loving surrender and service. They seek therefore to discern the Presence, not simply be themselves present. This is particularly important in formal relationships of spiritual direction. But spiritual development is also nurtured when friends seek to be attentive to God's presence in the lives of those for whom they care.

Attending to God's presence is a process of codiscernment. I do not simply point to God and pronounce, "There he is." Rather, I encourage my friend to seek to discern God's presence and call. This is particularly helpful when my friend feels God to be absent. Rather than try to convince him or her that God is present, it is usually much more effective for me to suggest that we pray together for help in discerning where God is in the situation.

Often we fail to discern God's presence because we look for him in the wrong places. Praying that we might know God's presence as we experience difficult circumstances is praying for new eyes that we might see him where he is, not where we expect him to be. Let me illustrate this with the story of John.

John struggled with depression. Not unexpectedly, when he became depressed he would feel that God had withdrawn from him. His cry of anguish matched that of Christ on the cross—"God, where are you when I need you?"

As we talked about this one day, I affirmed that his question was a good one. He seemed surprised. He thought it reflected a lack of faith. I told him that if he really meant the question and was willing to offer it as a prayer, I would join him in it as we together sought to discern the presence of Christ in his periods of darkness. I said that I was convinced that Christ was present at these times, and in fact *particularly* present then. But I also said that I suspected that God was not present in the way John expected. What we needed therefore was the gift of discernment—discernment of the hidden presence of Christ in John's suffering.

John was intrigued. After we talked about the matter a bit further, we prayed and agreed to get together for lunch in two weeks to see what progress he had made.

When we met, John told me that he had left our previous conversation with increasing doubt about what I had to say. However, he said, we had been good enough friends for long enough that he was willing to offer his next "Where are you God?" as a prayer rather than as an expression of anger.

Within a few days he again found himself slipping into a dark place. Instead of shaking his fist at the heavens because God had disappeared just when he most needed him, John dared to pray that God would help him believe that Christ was present with him in his darkness. He also asked for the gift of eyes to discern this presence.

What happened next was something that John did not anticipate. He reported that his depression continued to develop in much the usual way. However, there was one big difference—he did not feel alone. "Somehow the dark didn't feel as dangerous. I felt that although I could not see him, Jesus was there with me—hidden in the dark. Once I recognized that, I became sure he has always been with me in the darkness, perhaps standing right next to me. I just couldn't see him."

John still had many questions and continued to struggle. But he had made an important discovery. He was on his way to a new level of encounter with the hidden Christ who turns up where we least expect him and in forms that we often fail to recognize.

Learning to become aware of the presence of the Spirit lies right at the heart of growth in Christian spirituality. Apart from the Spirit there is no genuine Christian spiritual growth. Although there is obviously also an important place for the more active spiritual disciplines, spiritual growth begins with the easily overlooked disciplines of attentiveness and surrender.

The Gift of Dialogue

The core of the encounter with my friend was dialogue. Dialogue is one of the deepest forms of soul engagement we can experience with another person. It is a gift of inestimable value. Dialogue can never be manufactured, only nurtured and received with gratitude. And when we do receive the gift of meeting another person in a place of genuine dialogue, we participate in one of life's richest blessings.

Friends share what we generally call conversation. But not all conversation is worthy of being described as dialogue. Some conversation simply passes time—polite chitchat. Other things that we might describe as conversation involve a simple exchange of information—questions and answers. Still others are really more debates—all about winning and losing an argument.

Dialogue is richer than simple conversation, advice giving or communication. Dialogue involves shared inquiry designed to increase the awareness and understanding of all parties. In dialogue the intent is exploration, discovery and insight. In dialogue I attempt to share how I experience the world and seek to understand how you do so. In this process each participant touches and is touched by others. This results in each person's being changed.

In dialogue I meet you as a person, not an object. Objectification of people is the heritage of the professionalization of helping relationships. It is also the great enemy of distinctively Christian soul care. When we treat others as objects, even for benevolent reasons, we rob them of their humanity. The cardiologist who views her patient as "the man with arteriosclerosis" or the attorney who treats his client as "the woman with the messy divorce" have reduced the people they seek to help to a set of symptoms. This allows them to relate to them as objects of their professional expertise and avoid personal involvement. This may be fine for heart surgery and legal consultations, but it is absolutely untenable for soul care.

Martin Buber defined dialogue as an "I-Thou" encounter, in contrast to "I-it" encounters. In genuine dialogue I meet the other person as a "Thou"—someone worthy of respect and of getting to know. For Christians the possibility of dialogue begins with the recognition of others as persons made in the image of God. Seeing them in this sacred light makes it less likely that I will exploit them for my own interests. It also makes it more difficult for me to manipulate them, even for what I consider benevolent ends. Persons made in God's image deserve nothing less than respect, and respect is the foundation of dialogue.

I cannot imagine how I could offer sacred companionship to someone I did not respect. It seems to me that the best I could offer under these circumstances would be benevolence. But benevolence without respect is dehumanizing, because it reduces the other person to an object. Treating people as objects always robs them of some of their humanity. The recipients of benevolent objectification are well aware of this. If you doubt this, ask anyone who lives off the "charity" of handouts how it feels to receive such benevolence.

The precondition of dialogue is respect. Nothing helps me do this more than seeing the other person through the eyes of Christ. This is my prayer as I seek to relate to people I encounter in daily life. For when I see them through the eyes of Christ, I see their worth and dignity. I also see what they can become, not simply what they are. And if I am really willing to see them as God sees them, I see Jesus in them; I see them as imagers of the God who was fully represented in Jesus.

This is the great truth that Mother Teresa discovered as she spent her life serving the lowest of the low on the streets of Calcutta. Looking into the face of each person she encountered, she saw Jesus. This, she often said, made her acts of love easy. Seeing others with these eyes also transformed the vision of Peter Claver, a seventeenth-century Jesuit. Working with Africans who were victims of the cruelty of slave traders, Claver often took them into his care, offering his home and even his bed. On one occasion someone who was helping him ran from the room, panic-stricken before the disgusting sight of a particularly wretched-looking person. In astonishment and concern, Claver reportedly cried out: "You mustn't leave him, don't you know it is Christ!"

How could I fail to treat Christ with respect? How, then, can I fail to treat a person in whom Christ is present with the same respect? Respect is the foundation of dialogue, and Christians have a unique resource for offering it: eyes of faith that allow us to see those we encounter as deeply loved by God and bearing his image.

Describing the conversation of spiritual friends as dialogue should not make it sound as if they talk about only serious or religious matters. Nor is their conversation always intense. But describing it as dialogue reminds us that it is sharing of the soul. If my conversation never involves disclosing my deepest longings, anxieties or experiences of God, it cannot appropriately be called dialogue. Dialogue involves the risk of revealing what is most precious to me. If I remain in a safe zone of opinions, facts and information, I have not exposed my deepest self. Nor have I ventured to the place of deep encounter with others that is called dialogue.

Mediating Grace

Genuine dialogue is a sacred activity, because it is God's presence that enables us to meet another person in this deep, safe and intimate manner. Jesus promised that where two or three are gathered together in his name, he would be in their midst (Matthew 18:20). Genuine soul intimacy with others presupposes the presence of God. This is why attending to the Presence is so important in Christian spiritual friendships.

This is also why what I do or say is ultimately not all that important. The most important thing I can do is help the other person be in contact with the gracious presence of Christ. If I bring anything of value to the meeting, it is that I mediate divine grace. This is the core of Christian soul care. At their best, Christian friends help each other discern God's presence, recognize it as a presence of grace, come to trust that grace and surrender to it more fully.

Trusting and surrendering to grace is learning to say yes to God's yes to us. But first we must discern the grace in God's call to us. If we do not see grace—God's yes to us—we will never surrender to his will and his love. At the most we will offer obedience based on fear. A full-hearted, unqualified yes can come only in response to a discernment of the full-hearted, unqualified yes God extends to us.

Sacred friends mediate God's grace and help others recognize and respond to it. Put another way, they help each other discern and embrace God's will. But God's will for us is never that we simply comply with his desires. God's will is that we surrender to his love. Spiritual friends facilitate this surrender and in so doing facilitate Christian spiritual growth and transformation.

Reflecting on Hospitality, Presence and Dialogue

In this chapter I have focused on the primary gift that spiritual friends and directors give—the gift of their self. I suggested that this is more a gift of being than a gift of doing.

Hospitality is certainly something we can practice, but it springs naturally from the heart of the good host. The challenge is learning to be a good soul host. Soul hosts, I have argued, can offer hospitality to others because they have learned to offer hospitality both to themselves and to God's Spirit. Learning how to open themselves in quietness and surrender to the Holy Spirit, they are better able to open themselves to others. In doing so they offer a place of safety and belonging.

◉ Reflect on the quality of the soul hospitality that you offer yourself. How well cultivated is the quiet still center at the core of your own soul? What makes it difficult for you to be still in yourself?

◉ Reflect on the quality of the soul hospitality you offer the Spirit. What makes it difficult for you to be still in the presence of God? What makes it difficult for you to hear the still small voice of God in the quiet of your inner garden?

Part of the gift of soul hospitality is the gift of presence. Spiritual friends know how to make themselves available to others, temporarily setting aside their own preoccupations and distractions. They know how to genuinely be themselves and in so doing invite you to do the same. They really listen to you, opening themselves to your experience and receiving it as though it were their own. And because they themselves are growing in personal attunement to the Spirit of God, they know how to help you attend to God's presence.

◉ How would you assess the quality of the soul hosting you offer others? What gets in the way of your being genuinely present for others?

◉ Reflect on the way Jesus was present to those who he was with in the Gospels. Consider, for example, the way he encountered little children (Mark 10:13-16), the Canaanite woman (Matthew 15:21-28) or the rich young ruler (Mark 10:17-31). Place yourself in each of these stories as the person Jesus was with. What do you learn about how Jesus was present to people?

Finally, sacred companions know the blessing of dialogue—a concept I will say more about later. They have learned to receive dialogue as a gift, cherishing and nurturing it and never taking it for granted. And they have learned that where two or three are gathered together in Christ's name, he is in their midst. Spiritual dialogue is therefore prayer, a conversation in which the Holy Spirit is present as Christian friends mediate God's grace to each other.

❋ Reflect on the story of Jesus with the woman at the well (John 4:1-26) and see how it illustrates the principles of dialogue discussed in this chapter. What compromises the dialogue you experience with your most intimate soul friends? What would enhance it?

3

The Ideals
of Spiritual Friendship

*A*ccording to C. S. Lewis, friendship is one of the four basic human loves, the others being affection, eros and charity. Long overshadowed by romantic love, friendship is easily undervalued. The ancients viewed friendship as the crown of life, the fulfillment of all that is most distinctively human. Moderns all too often assess its value primarily in terms of its usefulness for achieving material ends (friends as business contacts) or minimizing boredom and loneliness (friends as people to kill time with).

The principal reason friendship is so undervalued is probably that too few people have ever experienced a significant, enduring friendship. All but the hermit have acquaintances. But typically such relationships involve no more than a passing connection. Most people also have colleagues with whom they work or associates with whom they spend regular time.

But this still falls short of the ideals of friendship. The coin of friendship has been continuously devalued by being applied to these lesser forms of relationship. Relationships between acquaintances or associates involve little of the intimacy, trust, commitment and loyalty of real friendships. Friendships may grow out of these more casual relationships but are not the same. Unfortunately, true friendships are also much more rare.

Friendship is one of God's special gifts to humans. Remarkably, *friendship* is one of the terms God uses to describe the relationship he desires with us. Friendship is therefore no ordinary relationship. We cheapen it when we reduce it to mere acquaintanceship. The ideals of friendship are worth preserving.

Model Friendships

The fact that friendship has its origins and foundation in the character of God makes it not surprising that the Bible is full of remarkable stories of friendship.

One of the greatest examples of a spiritual friendship in the literature of the West is the biblical account of the friendship of David and Jonathan. This story begins in 1 Samuel 18:1 (NIV) with the following disarmingly powerful words: "After David had finished talking with Saul, Jonathan became one in spirit with David, and he loved him as himself." Fourteen chapters later it ends with Jonathan's death and David's cry of anguish:

> O Jonathan, in your death I am stricken,
> I am desolate for you, Jonathan my brother.
> Very dear to me you were,
> your love to me more wonderful
> than the love of a woman. (2 Samuel 1:26)

These words were spoken by a man who knew the love of women. Recall David's lust-filled affair with Bathsheba, an illicit love that burned so strongly that it led David to murder her husband. But he recognized that the love he shared with Jonathan—each loving the other as himself—was a unique gift of wonder. As the story of that love unfolds, we see it expressed in acts of loyalty, enormous risk taking, tender devotion and, ultimately, a covenant of eternal friendship sworn in the name of the Lord and binding on their descendants for all time (1 Samuel 20:42).

The Old Testament book of Ruth tells another extraordinary friendship story—actually the story of two interlocking friendships. Ruth's remarkable friendship with her mother-in-law, Naomi, forms the foundation for the story and stands as a monument to the devotion of true friends. After Ruth has lost her husband, brother-in-law and father-in-law to death, Naomi urges her to return to her homeland and find another husband. This leads Ruth to assert her love for Naomi in the following familiar words:

> Do not press me to leave you and to turn back from your company, for
> wherever you go, I will go,
> wherever you live, I will live.
> Your people shall be my people,
> and your God, my God.
>
>
> Wherever you die, I will die
> and there I will be buried.
> May Yahweh do this thing to me
> and more also,
> if even death should come between us! (Ruth 1:16-17)

God honored Ruth's loyalty to her friend by introducing Boaz, a relation of her deceased husband, to the circle of friendship. What Boaz had heard of Ruth's faithfulness and kindness to her mother-in-law touched him, and he returned the gift of friendship to Ruth. This initially took the form of support and protection but eventually culminated in marriage.

The most remarkable biblical friendship story is that of Jesus and his disciples. This is particularly important for us, as it gives us a window to the relationship God claims to want with us. Not surprisingly, it also gives us one of the clearest biblical presentations of the ideals of friendship.

Jesus' relationship with his disciples begins, in each case, with his initiative. One by one, he invites them to follow him. This call was more than an invitation to belief or even to physical journeying together—it was a call to what I have described as the transformational journey of Christian spirituality. Although Jesus was clear about the costs of following him, the disciples could never have fully known the implications of their responding. It would forever change them and the world. Following Christ always has that implication.

Jesus' call was to journey with him. In addition to his emphasis on the costs of discipleship, he assured his disciples that he would never leave them alone, would share the intimacy he experienced with the Father with them, and ultimately would seal his friendship by laying down his life for them. He also assured them that if they did the will of his Father in heaven, they would be to him as his mother and brothers.

Jesus was not just talk. He did not just speak of friendship; he actually offered it to his disciples and followers. He

❋ spent time with them—eating, drinking, walking and discussing things that were important to both him and them (Luke 24:13-45)

❋ shared the most painful depths of his experience with them (Matthew 26:38)

❋ shared insights that were not disclosed to those outside the circle of friendship (Matthew 13:36-52)

❋ humbled himself in offering acts of tender care (John 13:1-17)

❋ offered them emotional support, repeatedly assuring them that there was no need for fear; and demonstrating genuine concern for their feelings (John 14)

❋ invited and answered their questions (Luke 9:18-27)

❋ related to them in ways that were loving yet challenged them to grow (John 13:1-17)

Reading the Gospels with a focus on the relationship between Jesus and the disciples is a powerful experience. Listen to Jesus' words to his disciples as you place yourself in their company:

A man can have no greater love
than to lay down his life for his friends.
You are my friends,
if you do what I command you.
I shall not call you servants any more,
because a servant does not know
his master's business;
I call you friends,
because I have made known to you
everything I have learned from my Father.
You did not choose me,
no, I chose you. (John 15:13-16)

These words are among the most amazing recorded in Scripture. Jesus, the Christ, the Son of God, invites us into the intimacy of the circle of friendship that exists between him and the Father. The friendship that Jesus offers he has shared from eternity within the Godhead. The Christian doctrine of the Trinity places friendship at the very heart of the nature of God. And almost unbelievably, the eternal interflow of companionship that binds Father, Son and Holy Spirit to each other extends to those Jesus calls to be his followers and friends.

Ideals of Spiritual Friendship
Five closely interrelated elements appear in the relationships between David and Jonathan; Ruth, Naomi and Boaz; and Jesus and his disciples. They are love, honesty, intimacy, mutuality and accompaniment. Let us look more closely at each of these ideals of spiritual friendship.

Love. Friendships involve a bond of love, never simply an obligation of love. Jonathan was described as loving David as himself and being one in spirit with him. This made his sacrifices and risks inconsequential.

True friends experience each other as being part of themselves in some profound way. Once I heard a woman describe such a friendship as involving the discovery of the other half of her soul. Plato used this same metaphor to characterize deep friendship: the experience of a single soul in two bodies.

Metaphorical allusions to being one in spirit or soul should not be interpreted so literally as to suggest that apart from such relationships we are missing half of our selves. But they do point toward the sense of deep connection that exists in friendships like David and Jonathan's. This connection involves much more than recognition of an overlap of interests or values. People can be similar in personality yet not experience any deep soul connection. They can also be different from each other yet experience a deep soul connection. Like Siamese twins connected in their bodies, soul friends are connected in the depths of their inner self.

According to C. S. Lewis, the bond of deep friendship involves the experience of another person as what he calls a "kindred soul." He suggests that kindred souls are people who see the same truth— or perhaps better, care about the same truth.[1]

Friendship involves passion. In contrast to romantic love, where the passion is between the individuals, in friendship the passion is shared in relation to something outside of the friendship. Friends share a love of at least one thing—be it ideas, politics, art or the spiritual journey. Apart from this there would be nothing for the friendship to be about. As noted by Lewis, those who have nothing can share nothing; those who are going nowhere can have no fellow travelers. The sense of being a kindred soul is therefore based on shared passion regarding important aspects of life.

While friends can be lovers and lovers should ideally be friends, Lewis notes some helpful contrasts between these two forms of love, if we do not push them too far apart. Speaking metaphorically, he suggests that whereas lovers stand gazing into each other's eyes, friends walk side by side in the pursuit of their shared interests. Lovers are always talking to each other about their relationship. In

---

[1]C. S. Lewis, *The Four Loves* (London: Fontana, 1960), p. 62.

contrast, friends hardly ever do so. Their focus is elsewhere—on the journey they share.

This is clear in the relationship between Jesus and the disciples. While the disciples were more than workers recruited to a cause, their focus was not just their friendship with Jesus. Jesus continually pointed them toward the will of the Father and the kingdom activities that were part of surrender to his will. Their friendship was not simply a feel-good mutual admiration society. It was built around knowing, loving and serving God.

Another important difference between friends and lovers is that friendship is much less vulnerable to jealousy. In contrast to romantic love, friends lose nothing by sharing their friends with others. There should be no place for exclusiveness in friendship. In fact, under normal circumstances, circles of friendship expand as other "kindred souls" are discovered, each addition to the circle enhancing, not diluting, the value of the network of relationships. Each person in the circle of friendship brings out particular aspects of the personality of each of the others. Each can thus be welcomed rather than warded off as a threat.

The inclusiveness of Jesus' friendship must have been difficult for the disciples to understand. They were used to friendships that were more exclusive, where the boundaries between inner and outer circles of acquaintances were clearer. Imagine their shock when after reprimanding the unknown man who was casting out demons, Jesus pronounced all who were not against him as for him (Mark 9:38-40). Imagine their shock when he welcomed sinners and outcasts into his circle of friendship. Imagine their shock when women were publicly included.

Friends show their love in an endless variety of ways. Undergirding these, however, is a central desire for the blessing of the other person. Friends long for each other's well-being and do whatever they can to support it.

In caring for me, my friends support my emotional, spiritual, intellectual and physical development. They do not simply want me to stay as I am. Rather, they seek my growth. They want me to become all I can be. They want me to develop my gifts and fulfill my potential. They want nothing less for me than that I become the full-orbed person I am called from eternity to be in Christ. They want nothing less than my wholeness and holiness. What a blessing it is to have even one such friendship!

It is important to note that friendship love is grounded in reality. This begins with the absence of idealization. The great weakness of romantic love is that lovers see each other through the unrealistic lens of idealization. This is, of course, why romantic love is unstable. Eventually reality always sets in and shatters the unrealistic perceptions of the loved one.

True friends, in contrast, see each other realistically. Because they know each other so well, they know the weaknesses that are hidden from the view of those at a distance. This awareness, however, does not diminish the respect, affection and admiration that they feel. But they are not prone to idolization. Friends are not fascinated by each other. Nor are they awestruck. They know each other not by the outer garb of persona but by the dependable and relatively stable elements of habit, character, disposition and trait. It is this down-to-earth quality of friendships that gives them stability and endurance. They may be unromantic, but they are anchored in reality.

One incident in the Gospel record of interactions between Jesus and his disciples is particularly striking in this regard. Matthew tells the story of how Jesus called him to disciple friendship, leaving his previous work as a tax collector. Tax collectors in first-century Palestine were notoriously corrupt and almost universally despised. So when Jesus went to Matthew's house for dinner and some of Matthew's fellow tax collectors turned up to meet his new friend, the Pharisees criticized Jesus for eating and drinking with sinners.

His response is instructive. Rather than defend Matthew and his friends, Jesus accepted their status as sinners. In fact he went further, identifying with them and declaring that it was sinners who were his priority and not the righteous, as it is the sick, not the healthy, who need a doctor (Matthew 9:10-13).

Such grounding in reality gives true friendships their enormous growth potential. Anything that calls a person to a firmer grasp on reality calls him or her to growth. There is no meaningful growth apart from solid reality contact.

One final aspect of friendship love that should be noted is loyalty. Jonathan's loyalty to David is at the core of the story's timeless appeal. The same is true of Ruth's loyalty to Naomi. Loyalty is always a gift of love. It is a gift, as it cannot be demanded. However, without it there is no real friendship—certainly nothing deserving to be called a spiritual friendship. Loyalty is given to the friend as an act of honor for the friendship and the friend.

Loyalty means faithfulness to commitments, spoken and unspoken. True friends preserve confidentiality, commit themselves to being honest with each other, avoid public criticism of each other and offer each other courtesy and respect. They carry their friends' best interests with them, always seeking to protect and advance them. They are also prepared to protect those interests, even at personal cost. Loyalty sometimes requires a sacrifice of self-interest. But this is a small price to pay for the priceless pearl of friendship.

Honesty. Because friends desire each other's growth and development, love demands honesty. It confronts illusions and dares to risk temporary discomfort by calling us to the truth.

Jesus' love for the disciples meant that he could not ignore some of the things he saw in them. When he predicted Peter's denial, he was not showing off his prophetic abilities; he was confronting Peter's pride. When he rebuked the disciples for their lack of trust in his ability to take care of them during a storm at sea, it was to encourage faith. And when he heard them arguing about which of them was greatest, his confrontation was motivated by desire for their spiritual well-being.

One particularly striking example of speaking the truth in love comes in the encounter between Jesus and Peter after Jesus' prediction of his own death. Peter protested, and Jesus spoke to him words that must have felt unusually harsh: "Get behind me, Satan! Because the way you think is not God's way but man's" (Mark 8:33). Did these words reflect a lack of care, or did they rather reflect deep love? Obviously the real lack of care would have been to overlook the triumphalistic assumptions that were lurking behind Peter's protest. It was love that motivated Jesus to confront Peter. Love cannot ignore things that are self-destructive in the loved one.

By daring to be honest with us, friends offer us invaluable opportunities for growth. They can help us penetrate our self-deceptions and cherished illusions. Just as the retina of the human eye contains a blind spot, so too the human soul contains a blind spot. Soul friends help us see things we cannot see on our own. There are things about ourselves that we would never recognize without them. The true soul friend will not accept our self-deceptions but will gently and firmly confront us with our soul blindness. Soul friends want each other to settle for nothing short of becoming the whole and holy person they are called to be.

When I reflect on how over the years my own friends have challenged me to grow, I recall numerous examples. Most of them relate to the personality thread that is my particular besetting sin. One good friend in high school confronted me on my arrogance. I deflected the confrontation. However, I took more note of it when another friend a few years later framed the same issue in terms of my detachment. Some years later my closest friend—my wife—prodded me to reflect on the anger that often seemed to lurk beneath the surface.

A pattern emerged, built around the dynamics of pride, detachment and feelings of entitlement. These dynamics are right at the center of the blind spot of my soul. They are sins I could not possibly see apart from the gentle confrontation of my friends.

While I was usually less open than I should have been to what these good friends offered me at the point of each confrontation, I owe them all an enormous debt of gratitude. My struggle in these areas continues. However, I would be at a much worse place than I am were it not for friends who have dared to offer loving nudges to growth. Nudges are never enough to ensure a response. They do, however, provide an opportunity.

When friends confront each other in these ways, they do so in love. This increases enormously the probability that the interaction will produce growth. If I suspect that my friend is merely attacking me, it is easy to ignore his or her challenge. However, when it's clear that my friend is pushing me simply because he or she loves me and wants me to grow, the confrontation is much harder to ignore.

The challenge is communicating love through a critical balance of support and confrontation. Confrontation without support will never be experienced as love. But support without confrontation will always remain an insipid form of love.

Friends communicate their love by offering emotional and spiritual support. This includes support for their friends' growth. However, that support will never be contingent on growth—withdrawn if I fail to make sufficiently good use of it.

Finally, honesty is not just something that friends try to practice. It is also something they delight in experiencing. The honesty that characterizes genuine and deep friendships is not just the honesty of words. It is also the honesty of being. Friends feel sufficiently safe with each other that they can relax and be what they are. Since I am already known and loved for who I am, pretensions can be set aside and I can be myself. Ralph Waldo Emerson describes a friend as a person with whom I can think aloud. This freedom from a need to manage appearances is a fundamental and basic component of all true friendships.

Intimacy. When people long for friendships that are more meaningful, they want someone with whom they can be known with the freedom and honesty I have just described. And they want to know the other person in the same deep ways. In short, they want intimacy.

Jesus' offer of friendship is an offer of intimacy. He wants to share our lives and share our experience. More remarkably, he invites us to share his life and his experience.

Consider how astounding it was that Jesus shared his anguish in the Garden of Gethsemane with the disciples (Matthew 26:36-46). First, note that he did not go to the garden alone. We might assume that his friendship with his Father would have been enough and that he would simply share his feelings with him in prayer. But no, he took three of his disciples when he went to this garden to deal with what he knew to be his imminent arrest and crucifixion.

Listen, then, to what he shared with them. The honesty and intimacy of the conversation is remarkable. He told them that his soul was bursting within him, overwhelmed with sorrow. And he told them he was close to not being able to take it any longer; he was at the point of death. Then he asked them to keep watch with him—to share his experience.

Intimacy is shared experience. Jesus shared his experience with those who were his closest friends. And he invited them to accompany him as he walked through this experience.

Intimacy can be experienced in a variety of forms. Two people are spiritually intimate when they share spiritual experiences, emotionally intimate when they share emotional experiences, sexually intimate when they share sexual experiences, and intellectually intimate when they share intellectual experiences. Other forms of intimacy include vocational intimacy (shared work), recreational intimacy (shared delight in play), creative intimacy (shared experiences of creating something), aesthetic intimacy (shared enjoyment of beauty) and social justice intimacy (working together to make the world a better place).

Spheres of intimacy reinforce each other. Friends who share intellectual discoveries become more deeply engaged with each other if they also share experiences that are political, spiritual or aesthetic. Couples who think intimacy is limited to sexual behavior know much less genuine intimacy than those who also share deeply on a broad range of other spheres of life. The deepest spiritual friendships are based on an ever-expanding range of spheres of intimacy.

This is most crucial in marriage, where it is easy to be intimate with one's spouse in one or two dimensions of life but outsource intimacy in other areas to friends. Many couples share sexual and emotional intimacy but very limited intellectual, aesthetic or spiritual intimacy. Dynamic spiritual friendships, particularly within a marriage, yearn for shared experience in a growing number of areas of life. The great danger of meeting too many of one's intimacy needs outside the marriage is that marital intimacy will, as a result, atrophy.

Like many other forms of relationship, friendships do not tend to remain static. They evolve or devolve—grow or shrink. If a friendship deepens over time, intimacy increases in depth and breadth. In fact, growth in intimacy is one of the best measures of growth in a friendship. In contrast, a sure sign of a dying friendship is a decrease of intimacy.

Spiritual friends share with each other at the level of their soul. This does not mean that they talk about only serious, personal or spiritual matters. However, if they never share at this level, the relationship is not worthy of being called a spiritual—or soul—friendship. Sharing at the level of their souls means that their intimacy is not restricted to experiences with the external world. Recall that *soul* refers to the whole person, with particular attention to one's inner life. Soul intimacy therefore is built upon sharing the inner self.

Friends who enjoy soul intimacy never settle for gossip or simple information exchange. Instead they use the data of events as springboards for the sharing of feelings, perceptions, values, ideas and opinions. The conversations of such friends are never merely about what happened in their lives or the world but move from this to how they experience, react to and understand what happened. Dialogue continually moves from the surface to the depths, from the external to the internal. This is the crucial distinctive of dialogue in spiritual friendships.

Spiritual intimacy demands this attentiveness to the inner world. Soul conversations invite inclusion of the spiritual dimension of life when they pay attention to inner experience, not simply the external world. Our spirituality is most clearly expressed in the deep longings that enliven us. Longings, in contrast to mere desires, come from our depths. Longings reflect spirit bubbling up to the surface—what we might theologically describe as a response of spirit to Spirit. Attending to the spiritual is attending to these stirrings in our depths.

Spiritual intimacy involves sharing these longings. It also involves sharing other aspects of inner experience neglected in more superficial exchanges—anxieties, hopes, concerns, dreams (both metaphorical and literal), preoccupations and ruminations. Things that might be counted as trivial are valued and shared because of this attentiveness to the inner world.

Most important, however, spiritual intimacy involves sharing our experience of God. I might tell my friend about a recent period of spiritual dryness in which God seemed absent. Or I might express gratitude associated with an answer to prayer. Or I might share an unusually strong sense of spiritual hunger.

This is not the same as discussing theology, church politics or even the Sunday sermon. Genuine spiritual intimacy involves sharing my experience, not simply my ideas. One component of this shared experience will usually be my experience of God.

The intimacy that exists between spiritual friends is a togetherness that honors separateness. I must never view my friend as an extension of myself—my property, my possession or someone who exists for me. This is the basis of the nonpossessiveness that should characterize spiritual friendships. Without an honoring of the separateness of each person, the intimacy of friendship is destructively symbiotic.

Honoring separateness removes some of the obligation that exists in other relationships. Friends owe nothing to each other except love. They are separate, autonomous people. Children and parents each owe the other a great number of things. Similarly, core obligations define the marital relationship. Friends have fewer formal obligations. Apart from love, they owe each other nothing. If they give more than they owe, this is a gift of grace.

Possessiveness always betrays a destructive dynamic in any relationship. The fruit of possessiveness is jealousy. Jealousy is as destructive in friendship as it is in marriage. Possessiveness, and the related dynamics of control and manipulation, always reflects an absence of respect for the separateness and autonomy of the other person.

It is important to remember that even the most intimate friendship cannot eliminate the strangeness that exists between any two people. The friend always remains partly stranger. It is naive to assume that two people can ever know each other completely. Real friendships acknowledge the mystery of the other person—a mystery that can at times delight and at other times disappoint. But it is this strangeness, this separateness, that keeps passion alive in a friendship. Space always nourishes genuine friendship.

A healthy friendship thus honors the space in the relationship. Each gives the other lots of room for friends, interests and experiences that form no part of the shared experience of the friendship. Such separateness is based on the awareness that my friend's life is not my life. His journey may connect to mine in some important ways, but because he is separate from me, his calling and journey are his own. As noted by Thomas Moore, "The soul . . . needs flight as much as it needs embrace."[2] Although we walk side by side, and at times hand in hand, we walk two separate and distinct paths. True friends never lose sight of this fact.

Mutuality. One important difference between friendship and other relationships of care is the presence of some degree of mutuality. One can offer support, counseling or ministry to someone

---

[2]Thomas Moore, *Soul Mates* (New York: HarperPerennial, 1994), p. 21.

who does not offer anything in exchange, but one can be a friend only to someone who offers the same in return. Friends offer each other what they receive from each other. This reciprocal nature of friendship marks it as distinct from all other relationships of care.

The mutuality that was present in Jesus' friendship with his disciples is truly remarkable. He did not invite them only to be followers but to be friends. And beyond this, he did not just offer to be their friend but invited them to be his.

Recognizing that friendships are supposed to be mutual and reciprocal, we feel betrayed and used when they are not. We complain when we are always on the giving end of a friendship, never on the receiving end. Such a relationship may have depth and significance and may be worthy of being called a relationship of soul care. But we set ourselves up for frustration when we view it as a friendship, for then we expect mutuality. It would be much better to view it as a relationship of ministry or service, in which I give care but do not expect any in return.

Viewing everyone to whom I extend Christian charity as a friend dilutes the concept of friendship. Similarly, viewing all relationships of pastoral care or Christian nurture as friendships introduces an element of dishonesty. Mutuality, at least at the levels experienced and expected by friends, does not form a part of most relationships of Christian ministry.

The mutuality of a friendship is based on a rhythm in which the giving and the receiving of each will balance over time, not within a given day or week or even month. But friendships are not primarily relationships of care. Primarily they are relationships of soul intimacy. Friends care for each other when this is needed, but that caring is not the only dimension of the relationship. If it becomes so, if the mutuality is lost, and if the shared exploration of the world that was originally motivated by being kindred spirits is missing, the relationship has shifted from a soul friendship to something else.

Mutuality does not mean equality. What Jesus offered the disciples was different from what the disciples offered Jesus. He was the spiritual teacher, they were the students. And yet he called them his friends. It was a relationship of intimacy and mutuality, even if it wasn't a relationship of equality. Much the same occurs in relationships of spiritual direction, the specialized form of spiritual friendship we will examine in later chapters.

Accompaniment. This brings us to the final ideal of friendship. Friends accompany each other on the journey of life.

The term *accompaniment* may have musical associations for you. These associations are actually quite relevant. One of my musician friends is an accompanist for recitalists. He tells me that the challenge the musical accompanist faces is not to lead or get in the road but to stay in close supportive contact with the person he is accompanying. The challenges in spiritual accompaniment are similar.

The first interactions between Jesus and his disciples recorded in Scripture were his invitations to join him on his journey. The wonderful thing about accepting this invitation was that he then accompanied them on *their* journey. And so it is with us. As Christ followers we participate in his life, but he also participates in ours. This is what true friends do. They accompany each other on life's journey.

Sometimes we are blessed with a friend who accompanies us for the whole of our adult life. Ruth and Naomi were blessed to be able to remain together, and one suspects that their friendship continued even after Ruth's marriage to Boaz. At other times the period of accompaniment is shorter. David and Jonathan journeyed together for only a small portion of David's life. But for however long they share friendship, true friends share enough of their separate journeys that these journeys become intertwined. Something that was separate becomes connected. My journey becomes our journey, and I am no longer alone.

Friends accompany each other by taking an active interest in each other's journey. As noted previously, this places a particular priority on the inner dimensions of that journey. But because the soul is the whole person, friends are also interested in the external aspects of each other's lives. Job frustrations, relationships with family members and other circumstances of life are shared and embraced with interest because true friends care for each other in their totality.

Because the accompaniment soul friends offer each other gives priority to the journey of the inner self, they can withstand physical separation. Even across the distance of times apart, friends can stay attuned to each other and continue to sense the flow of each other's lives. Catching up occurs quickly, and the connection seems never to have been interrupted. Accompaniment does not require a great deal of actual time together.

The lives of friends intermingle, and the intimacy they experience often spreads across a number of spheres of experience. They become an important part of each other's story because they share in important ways in each other's life. That sharing forms an important strand in the cord of accompaniment that binds their lives together. The friendship of Lynn and Angela nicely illustrates this.

Sisters in the Lord
Lynn is a single forty-four-year-old physician. Angela is married with two children. She is forty-six years old and works as an office manager. Angela's husband, Jerry, forms an important part of this relationship, so he should be introduced at this point as well.

Angela and Lynn first met at church. Discovering that Angela was seeking a job change, Lynn asked her if she would consider joining her family practice group as office manager. Angela took this job, reporting to Lynn, who served as the managing partner of the practice. She soon found her relationship to Lynn blossoming into a friendship.

Lynn was an only child who had always longed for a sister. Soon after Angela began to work for her, she sensed that Angela could become that longed-for sister. She remained cautious in her expectations, however, as Angela was married with two children and had a well-developed life of her own. However, Angela also clearly enjoyed the developing friendship. Her family of origin included several siblings of both sexes, but her family life was conflicted and dysfunctional. She too longed for a close relationship with a sister.

None of this was discussed between them until much later. The basis of the friendship was simply their enjoyment of each other's company. Increasingly, however, it also became the high degree of correspondence they discovered in their dreams and sense of calling.

Angela had a heart for service. She loved people and loved to serve them. Although she enjoyed office management and excelled at it, she wished that she had gone to college; if she had, she said, she would have wanted to train for one of the healthcare professions. She had the soul of a helper, and she longed to find ways to develop and use her gifts more fully.

Lynn's long-term objective was to serve people in less fortunate regions of the world. By the time she and Angela met, she had already done several short-term medical mission projects, and her dream was to do much more of this. She also dreamed of opening an inner-city clinic where she could serve the socially and economically disadvantaged. When she spoke of this with Angela, she discovered the depth of their shared passions.

From the beginning Jerry was highly supportive of his wife's friendship with her new employer. He sensed the importance of this friendship to Angela and repeatedly encouraged her to thank God for the good gift of the job and the friend and not worry about where it would lead. Jerry and Lynn also got along well. Soon Lynn was eating one meal a week at their home, and the three of them were becoming close.

The next summer Angela and Lynn went to the Philippines together on a two-week medical mission trip. This served to cement their relationship, and they returned with plans for the next trip. Soon this became an annual affair.

The really interesting and unusual aspect of this friendship is the presence of Jerry, the third party. Three-person relationships are often unstable. But after more than a decade this relationship appears solid. Jerry remains supportive of Angela and Lynn's special friendship. Lynn has always been respectful of Jerry and Angela's marriage. And Angela takes care to ensure that Jerry has no reason to feel jealous or resentful. Although the friendship between Angela and Lynn is what most people notice, the three of them also have a remarkable friendship. They have vacationed as a threesome on a number of occasions, and Jerry has twice accompanied Angela and Lynn on their annual mission trips. The primary relationships remain, however, the marriage and the friendship of Angela and Lynn. Each seems supportive of the other, adding value, not detracting.

Growing Together

The network of relationship between Angela, Jerry and Lynn reminds us that the ultimate test of a spiritual friendship is whether all parties are growing as a result of it. Intimate relationships can be either soul-destroying or soul-nurturing. Soul-nurturing friendships include increasing levels of

- attunement to the Spirit, hunger for God and surrender to his will
- love for others
- self-understanding and attentiveness to the voices of my inner world
- curiosity about God's creation
- enjoyment of life
- discernment of my unique self-in-Christ
- courage to follow my calling
- depth of passion and compassion
- sense of gratitude
- overall experience of holiness and wholeness

However, since none of us exists in only a single relationship, another question to be asked of any friendship is what its impact is on other relationships. For married couples, all other relationships need to be evaluated against the criterion of how they affect the marriage. For singles, the question is how the friendship affects other intimate relationships. For the Christian, this includes our relationship with God.

Every relationship we experience, particularly every significant relationship, changes us in important ways. The question is, do those changes aid our growth or hinder it? Is the overall impact of the relationship on my spiritual journey positive or negative? The possibility for both exists.

Soul Friendships with Non-Christians

Out of a fear of the potential adverse effect on their spiritual life that a close friendship with a non-Christian might have on them, some Christians avoid soul intimacy with spouses or acquaintances who are not Christians. Others avoid it simply because they believe it is not possible to meet people in places of soul intimacy apart from a shared-faith journey. Both understandings are, from my point of view, tragically incorrect.

While the most intimate forms of spiritual friendship described in this chapter are restricted to those on a similar spiritual journey, there is no question that our shared humanity allows us to experience deep soul connections with others. All that is required is that we meet in places of depth, honesty and mutual respect.

Too often I have seen husbands and wives who desperately long for soul intimacy cross their spouse off the list of eligibility because she or he is not a Christian. Sadly, both experience loneliness, rejection and anger as a result.

What a transforming gift it can be to such husbands and wives when they learn to entrust their spouse with their inner world. This must never be done as a strategy to manipulate them into change. Rather it must be offered as an invitation to meet in soul intimacy at a place of shared humanity.

I have seen wonderful friendships flourish when a Christian

accepts a non-Christian partner as he or she is and seeks to build soul intimacy. This will never happen quickly. In fact, depending on the history of the relationship, initial overtures may be rejected and mistrusted. But soul hospitality can transform a relationship. And it can transform both parties to the relationship. It must, however, be offered as an invitation, not a strategy of manipulation. And invitations can be rejected. They carry no guarantees.

This applies equally to nonspousal friendships. Good potential soul friendships should never be spurned simply because the other person is not on the same spiritual journey or not at the same place on the journey.

Grace and the Space Between Ideals and Reality

The ideals of friendship should not be confused with reality. In the real world friends fail each other, seek to control each other, feel possessiveness and jealousy, experience limitations in their love, and lack courage for honesty and intimacy.

The failures in the inner circle of Jesus' friends were spectacular. In spite of his best intentions and resolve, Peter denied Christ. Fear was stronger than loyalty. And Judas, whom Jesus called "friend" even at the moment when he came to betray him, was anything but a true friend.

When I think of my own closest friendships, I realize how far short of the just-discussed ideals I routinely fall. My love is limited by my inability to set aside self-interest, my honesty by my abundant and endlessly creative self-deceptions, my intimacy by my fear, genuine dialogue by my egocentricity and respect for separateness by my need to control.

But true friendships do not demand perfection. We come to them as we are and are received with grace by someone who accepts and loves the imperfect self we bring. There is, after all, no other self we can bring. Either our friend accepts us as we are, or we are forced to do the same posturing that characterizes our other relationships. The great gift of genuine friendship is that it allows us to live in the space between ideals and reality.

Reflecting on the Ideals of Spiritual Friendship

This chapter began with a review of several biblical examples of friendship. But friendship is even more central to the Bible than these examples might suggest. Friendship has its origin and meaning in the intimacy of the eternal circle of friendship that exists within the Godhead.

If God did not experience eternal friendship within the Trinity, we would never have known the possibility of this gift of soul intimacy. Remarkably, it is this friendship that God invites us to join. This friendship forms the prototype for all human friendships.

✦ Reflect on the friendship that has been shared from eternity between God the Father, God the Son and God the Holy Spirit. Now allow yourself to imagine the day that God decided to create humans and to invite them into this circle of friendship. As you meditate on this, allow yourself to respond to God in prayer with gratitude. How does recognizing this source of human friendship change your understanding of the ideals of friendship?

Spiritual friends participate in the divinely inspired pattern of intimacy by sharing themselves and their experience. Spheres of intimacy reinforce each other and tend to either expand or contract.

✦ Think about your marriage or closest friendship and identify the spheres of intimacy you experience (sexual, spiritual, intellectual, aesthetic, recreational, vocational and so on). How has the nature of your intimacy changed over the past year? What challenges and opportunities do you see in this relationship?

✦ Reflect on the spiritual intimacy you experience in your most important friendships. Do these friendships offer you a place to share regularly the stirrings of your soul? How well do you create a space where others are encouraged to share their inner journey? What makes it difficult for you to help others move from a focus on the external world to a focus on their inner experience?

Of course friendships do not always live up to the ideals. Tragically, the actual experience of friendship often leads to disillusionment and disappointment.

▨ Reflect on significant friendship failures you have experienced. What have you learned about yourself from these experiences? How have they influenced the way you approach friendships now? If your enthusiasm for spiritual friendship needs bolstering, meditate on the biblical examples of friendship listed earlier in the chapter.

If you are blessed to have one or more genuine spiritual friendships, be sure to thank God, because such friendships are not an entitlement but a gift. Christ, who said to his disciples, "You have not chosen me, but I have chosen you," might say of Christian friends, "You have not chosen each other, but I have chosen you for each other."

Spiritual friendship is not a reward for good behavior. It is the means by which God reveals his goodness by helping us know others and ourselves and thereby know him. It is a gift God gives to us. It is a gift we can give to others.

Part Two

SPIRITUAL DIRECTION

4

Demystifying
Spiritual Direction

*U*ntil recently most Protestants have been unfamiliar with the concept of spiritual direction. Those who have heard of it often equate the notion with submission to a religious authority and view it with misgiving. Others associate it with counseling, perhaps thinking of it as the most recent fad in a field often associated with new techniques and approaches. A few people realize that spiritual direction is ancient rather than new and that it has nothing to do with authority, but they incorrectly assume that it is relevant only to those pursuing a professionally religious calling.

All of these reactions are based on serious misunderstandings. Spiritual direction, the jewel in the crown of soul-care relationships, has been an important part of formal relationships of Christian nurture since the earliest days of the church. Rather than being for a specialized few, it is highly relevant to every Christian who takes the spiritual journey seriously. Rather than being a relationship of authority, it is a form of spiritual friendship. And although it shares some features with counseling and other relationships of care, it is distinct from all of them—serving more as an alternative to Christian counseling than a component of it.

But before looking more carefully at what spiritual direction is and is not, consider several examples of this rich and diverse form of Christian spiritual nurture.

Sita goes to see her pastor once a month for spiritual encouragement. She does not have any particular problem for which she seeks help. She merely values a brief time of shared prayer and conversation about how she is progressing on her spiritual journey. Neither she nor her pastor thinks of what they do as spiritual direction. Her pastor might describe it as pastoral care. Sita simply thinks of it as spiritual support.

Bill is a pastor who has struggled to find a way to balance church growth and spiritual growth in his ministry. Six months ago he attended a weekend retreat that included a time for brief conversation and prayer with the retreat director. Since then he has continued to meet periodically with this person, their conversation focusing on Bill's prayer life. He deeply values these meetings, as they are the one place he feels completely free to be himself. He also appreciates the fact that he has no obligation to minister to his spiritual director. This relationship is for him.

Paul has been meeting for prayer and conversation with his friend Matt since they were in a Bible study together several years ago. They meet twice a month in a quiet corner of a coffee shop before work. The pattern of what they do has evolved over time; they currently use one meeting a month to focus on Paul and his journey, and the other on Matt. They describe the value of the experience in terms of encouragement and accountability. Since they are in the same church, they meet in other contexts as well. However, their first- and third-Tuesday morning meetings are unique and kept separate from other encounters. This time they keep special by ensuring that it is focused on their spiritual journey.

Maria meets once a month with an older Christian woman whom

she has always respected for her spiritual maturity. It began as informal conversations after the Sunday service. Maria often told her friend about her spiritual struggles. While the woman was reluctant to offer advice, she obviously cared deeply for Maria and always assured her that she would pray for her. Recently they have begun to get together for lunch and more extended conversation. The pattern of their interaction remains much the same, although it now always includes a brief time of prayer.

What Spiritual Direction Is Not

Spiritual direction is not mysterious. It does not involve secret handshakes or esoteric rituals. It is not very different from some of the things Christians currently do as they seek to nurture spiritual growth in each other. But neither is it many of the other things people associate it with. Being clear about what it is not is the first step toward understanding what it is.

Spiritual direction is not new. Christian spiritual direction goes back to the earliest days of the church, and its practice in Judaism and other religions was well established before that. Letters of spiritual guidance were a primary means of providing spiritual direction in the first-century A.D. and are preserved for us in the New Testament in the form of the Epistles. The desert fathers of the fourth and fifth centuries provided spiritual counsel to thousands of Christians who, seeking increased personal holiness, visited them in the deserts of the Middle East. Through their writings these wise Christians continue to guide many, even in our own century.

The Protestant Reformers were all active in providing spiritual direction to others. Martin Luther did most of this by means of correspondence, much like the apostle Paul fourteen centuries earlier. Ulrich Zwingli, while recommending confession of sins to God alone, urged Christians to consult other wise and mature Christians for assistance on the spiritual journey. And John Calvin, while stressing that the individual Christian's subservience should be to

God alone, offered spiritual direction and proclaimed its merits.

This makes the subsequent decline of interest in spiritual guidance among Protestants somewhat surprising. However, with emphases on the priesthood of all believers and preaching as the primary means of spiritual nurture, spiritual direction was viewed with increasing suspicion. This has begun to change in the past several decades as evangelicals have experimented with forms of shepherding and discipleship, and even more recently as large numbers of Protestants have opened themselves to discover the riches associated with the classical spiritual disciplines.

Spiritual direction is not authoritarian. Much of Protestants' historic suspicion about spiritual direction is related to the misunderstanding of the place that authority plays in it. The term *direction* implies telling someone what to do. The fear is therefore that people seeking help place themselves under the authority of the spiritual director, submitting passively to the direction provided. While spiritual direction may have been practiced in this way at some points in the past, it is not generally so now.

It is important to distinguish spiritual direction from shepherding. Shepherding, a somewhat autocratic form of spiritual leadership prominent in some denominations in recent decades, has virtually nothing in common with spiritual direction.

Spiritual direction should never involve a replacement of divine authority with human authority. It does not place an intermediary between the individual and God. The only authority that has any place in spiritual direction is God himself and his Word. The true spiritual director is the Spirit of God.

Spiritual direction is the facilitation of attunement to God. It is in no way similar to orders given by a military captain to a soldier. Rather, it is one Christian accompanying another as he or she seeks to increase attentiveness to the presence and direction of the Spirit of God.

Spiritual direction is not giving advice. Some people are attracted to spiritual direction with the hope that someone they trust will tell them what to do to get their spiritual life on track. Perhaps they feel overwhelmed or stuck on the spiritual journey. Or perhaps they simply feel nothing spiritually.

All of these are good reasons to seek spiritual direction. However, you should not expect a spiritual director to tell you what to do. If this is really what you seek, a relationship of pastoral counseling (or what is sometimes called biblical counseling) might be more appropriate.

Spiritual directors may offer suggestions or ideas, but their job is not to give either advice or direction. That remains the role of the Holy Spirit—the true spiritual director.

Spiritual direction is not discipling. Spiritual direction also differs in important ways from discipling relationships. Although the term *discipling* is used in a variety of ways, it generally implies more accountability on the part of the one seeking help and more direction being given by the one offering help. While spiritual direction may involve a degree of accountability, it is primarily a relationship of accompaniment. And while spiritual directors may at times direct the process of the discussion, they are much less likely to direct the content. They are also more likely to offer suggestions than to give advice.

Discipling is also more structured than spiritual direction. It often involves following some curriculum of instruction. Spiritual direction, in contrast, involves no standardized curriculum or preconceived plan on the part of the spiritual director.

Finally, as noted earlier, discipling tends to focus on the early steps of the Christian spiritual journey. The metaphor of helping people become disciples is rich and can—broadly understood—be applied to any relationship of Christian spiritual nurture. However, as usually understood it refers specifically to helps given to those new in the faith as they seek to acquire the foundational disciplines of the Christian life. In contrast, spiritual direction is most helpful for those who have already acquired the basic disciplines of the Christian life.

Spiritual direction is not preaching. Just as spiritual direction does not involve telling someone what I think they should do, neither does it involve telling them what I think God thinks they should do. It is a relationship neither of proclamation nor of exposition.

The spiritual director does not function like a preacher, seeking to challenge, exhort, edify or direct another person by expounding God's Word. While Scripture may play a role in the relationship, "thus said the Lord" sorts of pronouncements have no place in it.

In general, spiritual direction is more Spirit-centered than Word-centered. The focus is on God himself. Discerning the presence and leading of the Holy Spirit is the central task.

Spiritual direction is not moral guidance. More surprising, perhaps, is the fact that spiritual direction is not primarily a matter of offering moral guidance. In general, morality is not the primary concern of this form of Christian nurture. The primary concern is deepening one's relationship with God.

Morality forms such a deep and foundational aspect of personhood that moral considerations will generally be addressed in any significant soul dialogue. Also, because sin interferes with our relationship with God, seeking ways to deepen that relationship will often lead to an encounter with sin. However, to restrict spiritual direction to moral guidance severely limits its scope. And being preoccupied with moral considerations keeps us from being properly preoccupied with the Spirit of God, whose agendas for personal transformation are often not ours.

Spiritual direction is not counseling. Counseling and spiritual direction share some common features but differ in very important ways. The most important of these differences is that while counseling is problem-centered, spiritual direction is Spirit-centered. Although spiritual direction could theoretically be initiated by a crisis or problem, its goal is growth in one's relationship to God, not resolution of particular problems. The problem, if there is one, is merely the place where one can expect to meet God. Other than that, it is not the focus.

Another important difference from counseling is seen in the role of empathy in the relationship. Counselors seek to be empathic to the inner experience of those they counsel. Spiritual directors, on the other hand, make their empathic focus not primarily the other person but the Spirit. This means that the spiritual director's goal is not primarily to understand how the person seeking direction feels. Nor is it to enter the person's experience and see the world as he or she does. Rather, it is to help the person come more closely in touch with the Spirit of God. As we will see subsequently, the empathic focus of the director is not primarily the other person but the Spirit of God.

A final difference between counseling and spiritual direction is that whereas note taking and record keeping are generally understood to be important in clinical therapeutic relationships, most spiritual directors judge them to have no place in spiritual direction. I concur with this judgment. Record keeping makes the encounter overly clinical. It also shifts the focus of the director from God to the person he or she is seeking to accompany.

Spiritual direction is not teaching. Finally, spiritual direction is not focused on content in the way teaching is. There is no curriculum to cover. Nor is spiritual direction's success to be judged in terms of understanding of concepts or orthodoxy of theology. While learning obviously forms an important part of the relationship, it is much more a matter of learning of love and surrender than a learning of articles of faith. And it is much more a matter of colearning than of an expert imparting skills or knowledge to a novice.

In this process of colearning, spiritual directors function like guides more than teachers. They accompany others on the journey not as experts but as companions. Having escorted others on similar journeys, they are sometimes in a position to offer assistance in selecting the best route. Furthermore, because they know the region where you and they are journeying, they may be able to help you put the journey in perspective—to see where you are in terms of where you are going. But the way they best facilitate the learning that is important to the spiritual journey is by continually orienting themselves and you to the Spirit.

What Spiritual Direction Is
I propose to define spiritual direction as follows:

Spiritual direction is a prayer process in which a person seeking help in cultivating a deeper personal relationship with God meets with another for prayer and conversation that is focused on increasing awareness of God in the midst of life experiences and facilitating surrender to God's will.

Let us briefly examine the four basic components of this definition before we consider how they come together in real life.

Spiritual direction is a prayer process. Prayer is central to spiritual direction. I do not mean that spiritual direction involves talk about prayer. Nor do I mean that it occasionally involves actual prayer. What I mean is that it is, or becomes, prayer.

I understand prayer as attunement and response to God's presence. It is becoming conscious of the fact that I am in God's presence. It is learning to be attentive to this presence and responding to it in worded and unworded ways. Conversation with another person who seeks to heighten attentiveness to God's presence *is* prayer. When Jesus promises that where two or more people are gathered in his name he is present with them, that means the conversation of two is actually a conversation of three. Conversation becomes prayer when both the director and the directee are aware that they are in God's presence.

Regardless of whether eyes are closed or words are being spoken, spiritual direction is prayer when both the director and the directee seek to be attentive to the presence of God and respond to that awareness. Prayer is central to spiritual direction because it keeps both participants focused on God.

Spiritual direction is help in cultivating a deeper personal relationship with God. The goal of spiritual direction is the deepening of one's relationship with God. Spiritual directors do not produce a relationship between the directee and God. But they do seek to foster the development of such a relationship.

Spiritual direction involves a set of relationships between three persons—the director, the directee and God. Central to this is not the relationship between the director and the directee but between the directee and God. This is different from counseling, where the relationship between the counselor and counselee is of primary importance. Spiritual directors must avoid overvaluing their relationship with those they seek to help. The relationship of primary importance is the relationship between the one seeking spiritual direction and the Lord. Next in importance is the relationship between the director and God.

Taken together, the relationships of each party to God form the twin foundations of the relationship between the director and the directee. These two primary relationships allow the encounter between the director and directee to facilitate the directee's personal relationship with God.

This is very significant. If the director thinks that his or her relationship with the directee is the crucial matter in spiritual direction, both director and directee are in serious trouble. The director should fade into the background. The crucial presence is God's presence. The crucial relationship is the personal relationship of each to God.

Spiritual direction is focused on increasing awareness of God in the midst of life experience. The primary focus of spiritual direction is experience, not theology. While priority is given to spiritual experience (that is, awareness of God), the initial focus is experience in general. The reason for this is that the search for God in the midst of everyday experience is the beginning of a life of attunement to his presence. Attunement to God's presence is the core of prayer and the royal route to a deeper relationship with him.

Paying attention to God is at the core of spiritual direction. Spiritual directors seek to help us attend to the God who continuously reaches out to us. The Christian God is a God of revelation. He has revealed himself in Christ, he reveals himself in Scripture, and he reveals himself in his world. But the transcendent God who becomes immanent also meets us in our inner world. He speaks to us in the still quiet places in our soul. To hear his voice, however, requires both discernment and moving from self-absorption to God absorption.

Self-absorption is the great enemy of attunement to God. This is why anything that breaks self-absorption can facilitate attentiveness to God. Music, walks in the woods or meditation on great works of art can all play important roles in this. This is not because God is in such experiences in some special way. Rather, it is because such experiences help us move from self-absorption. This is always the first step toward God absorption.

God constantly reaches out, seeking our attention, seeking to be known. We walk through his world oblivious, failing to notice him. We are so wrapped up in ourselves—our plans, our worries, our activities—that we fail to see him. Anything that helps us develop a receptive posture of openness to the Divine prepares us to encounter the God who constantly reveals himself.

Spiritual direction seeks to cultivate a climate of attention to and reflection on experience—particularly focusing this attention on an effort to discern the presence and leading of God's Spirit in our life. Prayerful attentiveness is an integral part of this process.

Spiritual direction is directed toward surrender to God's loving will. Finally, the goal of attending to the presence and leading of God's Spirit in our life is surrender to his love and his will for us. It is not sufficient simply to discern God's call and presence. God wants us to surrender to his love. Apart from this he cannot be fully known. And it is only in this knowing of God that authentic transformation is possible.

But surrender to God's love is surrender to his will. Apart from a surrender to his love, obedience will remain an act of duty, never an expression of devotion. God wants more than obedience. He also wants our love. Spiritual direction seeks to facilitate a surrender to God's love that expresses itself in choosing his will over ours.

An Illustration

Let us return to the earlier story of Bill to better understand how this works in a real relationship. Recall that Bill was a pastor who sought a deeper personal experience of God as he struggled to balance church growth and spiritual growth in his congregation. He had attended a retreat led by my wife and me, and subsequently contacted me to see if I would be willing to offer him spiritual direction.

Bill was already well advanced on the Christian spiritual journey. He was the pastor of a successful church and widely recognized as a man of spiritual maturity and wisdom. For many years he had also been heavily involved in providing others with a form of spiritual direction he called mentoring. He told me, however, that he felt dissatisfied with his own spiritual life. He wanted help in encountering God more deeply in prayer.

I felt intimidated. What could I teach him about prayer? He had probably preached more sermons on prayer than I had ever even heard. Furthermore, he held two degrees in theology. In contrast, I had no formal theological training.

The idea of my helping him learn to pray seemed laughable. I wanted to ask him to help me with *my* prayer life! I told him so. This turned out to be an excellent thing to do, as it allowed him to help me get my role back into perspective. It was the first sign of the collaborative nature of the venture we were about to undertake.

Bill told me that he was not looking for a spiritual guru who would teach him advanced techniques of prayer. Nor did he expect me to tell him what to do. Rather, what he wanted was someone with whom he could meet, pray and discuss his prayer life. He wanted someone who would provide spiritual accompaniment, not specialized spiritual expertise.

My sense of spiritual inadequacy in guiding others on the spiritual journey serves me well. It keeps me focused on the fact that it is the Spirit who is the true spiritual director. I am merely his assistant. Remembering that does a great deal to remove the pressure to perform.

Session one. Although I knew Bill somewhat from the retreat we had done together, I began our first session by asking him to tell me what he wanted from the Lord and from spiritual direction. I also asked him to tell me about his deepest longings. Recall that longings are the breath of the soul. They reflect our spiritual health and appetites. They also usually reflect something of the call of Spirit to spirit.

Bill told me how much he desired deeper intimacy with God. He told me how the retreat had helped him begin to sense God's presence throughout his day but how much he longed to have this awareness fill his consciousness. He said that what he needed was what he would call an urban spirituality—a spiritual experience not of the mountaintop but of the city. He wanted a sense of God's presence that wasn't limited to times of prayer but that would be with him throughout the day, regardless of where he was or what he was doing. He wanted increased God consciousness.

We spent about twenty minutes talking about these matters. I then suggested that we had a chance right in this moment to begin to work toward what he desired. I asked him about his experience of God's presence as we were speaking.

He replied, "This is a good example of what I have been trying to describe. I'm talking about God, but I can't say that I have any direct sense of his presence. I know God must be present, but I base that more on belief than experience."

"What are you aware of?"

"My questions about how I should experience God. I guess it makes me wonder how realistic my expectation about God consciousness really is."

"Okay," I said, "but instead of focusing on your feelings or your questions, focus on where God might be in your present experience. You said you believe he is present. Let's pray together that you will be able to discern where he is in your present experience."

We briefly prayed this prayer together, he first and then I. After a few moments of silence he said, "You know, I think I do feel his presence. He is in my desire."

"Tell me more," I said.

"Well, I think he is in my longing for him. My desire is from him; so it reflects his Spirit. And if it reflects his Spirit, it reflects his presence."

"I believe you are absolutely right. But notice that you don't base this on a feeling but on an awareness."

"You're right, and I think that is an important point. I think I judge his presence by feelings—spiritual feelings, but feelings nonetheless. But I also wonder if God is more easily seen in the past than in the moment. Just as I was able to sense his presence only when I stopped and stood back from my immediate experience, so I wonder if he intends us to see him when we cast our eyes back over the past rather than in the midst of the experience."

"That may be," I said, "but you say that what you want is a sense of his presence within the moment—during the day, not just at the end of the day when you look back."

"Yes, that is exactly what I want. And I want to believe that it is possible. Brother Lawrence *[The Practice of the Presence of God]* seems to suggest it is, as do many other spiritual writers. I just don't know how to make it my experience."

I asked him to tell me more about when he had a clear sense of God's presence. He told me about his experience of God when he was preaching. He also told me that he was often aware of God's presence in nature and that he loved to take walks in the botanical gardens near his church when he had time. He returned once again, however, to his frustration over his inability to experience God in the same way during the course of his day. He again asked if I thought his expectations were realistic.

I hesitated. I did not know how to answer. My own experience of

God during the day was still limited. But I didn't want to use my experience as a reference point. Others, I knew, were able to experience God's presence much more than I. Should I encourage him on the basis of this? Or should I share my own experience? Or, perhaps, should I avoid the question since we were nearing the end of our time?

I chose to tell him that I planned to avoid the question, at least for the moment. I told him that I didn't think I was in a position to judge the realism of his desire. But, I suggested, the Spirit could. I asked if he had made that question a matter of prayer. He said that he hadn't but would like to.

We were nearing the end of our time. I asked if he was open to a simple exercise that might be of help in discerning God's presence. He said he was.

I suggested that he take ten minutes at the end of each day for a prayerful review of the day. In particular, he could note when God seemed present, when he seemed absent, and when he might have been present but it was not obvious. I then suggested that Bill conclude this time with a prayer of thanksgiving for the times when he sensed God's presence and with a petition for spiritual discernment that he might better be able to discern God's presence the next day. I suggested that he record these reflections in his journal and bring it to our next meeting, in three weeks.

Session two. Bill began our next session by telling me that the exercise had not worked well for him. He said he found the evening reviews to be frustrating as he was forced to rely on his beliefs, not experience. I asked him what that meant; he elaborated.

"Well, I know God must be present, and I have never really doubted that. But in most of the experiences of my day I can't say I sense his presence. Not in the way I do when I am preaching. Nor even in the way I do when I am counseling someone and silently praying for help in knowing what to say."

"What tells you God is present in those moments?" I asked.

"Mostly a sense of his power. I feel anointed, filled with his Spirit.

You must know what I'm talking about."

"I think I do," I replied. "But I wonder if you are expecting God to appear to you in the same way under all circumstances and if you are missing his presence because sometimes he is not in the wind or earthquake or fire but in the still small voice. You told me that for a long time your prayer has been that you would have power in ministry. I believe God has granted that. But perhaps your difficulty in sensing God's presence is related to your expecting him to always come to you in power. If so, that would make it hard for you to discern his presence when he appears in weakness, brokenness, poverty or stillness."

This seemed to strike a chord with Bill. He talked about how much he longed to be used by God but how much he associated that with power. He admitted that he would have a difficult time feeling that God was using him if his ministry was not overtly successful. He found that difficult to confess, but it seemed related to the notion that he expected to meet God in places of power.

He also recounted an interesting experience. The previous year he had visited another church on Good Friday. Participating in an ecumenical service in his community, he had been troubled by what he perceived as a depressive quality to the service. In his mind it had left Christ in the tomb, without any hint of what was to come on Easter morning. He was accustomed to connecting the themes of the two days much more closely, and he found the space created by this service between Good Friday and Easter Sunday moving. It had led him to wonder whether he was missing something of the joy of the resurrection by minimizing the despair of the crucifixion.

Bill's ruminations continued for some time. I interrupted by asking about his sense of God's presence in our current conversation.

"I know God is present because I am convinced there is some truth to what we are exploring. I believe we are being led by the Spirit of Truth."

"I agree," I said. "Why don't you just close your eyes and sit quietly for a moment and listen to what the Spirit is saying to you? Don't worry about saying anything in response. Just listen."

He closed his eyes and sat in silence for several moments. With his eyes still closed, he began to pray: "Speak, Lord, for your servant is listening."

We remained in silence. After a few more moments he opened his eyes and spoke to me. "It's so hard to sit quietly before God. I fill the space between us with words. But when I stop my incessant nattering, I do sense God's presence. It is quite wonderful."

He then asked me how I had learned to be still before God.

"With great difficulty," I replied. "I am far from an expert on stillness." I then told him something of my own struggles with being still and of the unfortunate spiritual consequences of this soul restlessness.

But I also spoke with him of the help I had been receiving from work with what is known as "centering prayer." Briefly I described this approach to prayer as learning to sit quietly in God's presence, focusing myself on him and gently returning my attention to him by saying his name whenever I find my mind drifting to other things. I told him how this had begun to bear fruit for me, as the Spirit was teaching me to relax in God's presence and not work so hard at consciously focusing on him or even thinking about him. Bill knew of centering prayer from our retreat together but took note of a book by Basil Pennington[1] that he said he would like to read and discuss further at some later point.

We concluded this second time together with further prayer. I suggested that he continue the practice of ending his day with a review of God's presence during the day, and we arranged the next time to meet.

These few moments from my work with Bill should not be taken

---

[1]Basil Pennington, *Centering Prayer* (New York: Image, 1982). See also my "Suggestions for Further Reading" at the end of this book for additional resources in this prayer tradition.

as a model of what spiritual direction should be. But hopefully they illustrate something of what it is and what it is not.

Had I been functioning as a counselor, I would have worked harder to identify a problem and focus on it. I might have concluded that the "problem" with which he needed help was his difficulty in sensing God's presence. My job, then, would be to fix this problem—to do something to help Bill better sense God's presence.

But to turn his desire for deeper intimacy with God into a problem would be to focus on something that needed to be fixed. And to make it my job to change something in Bill would be to miss the point that it is the Holy Spirit—not I—who initiates and sustains all growth. Spiritual direction does not attempt to "fix" things. Rather than focus on problems, it focuses on spiritual longings. Instead of being reparative, it is developmental.

If I had approached my work with Bill as a teacher, I would have focused on communicating principles and teaching skills that would be relevant to his desire for deeper experience of God. But the focus of spiritual direction is neither content nor skills. The focus of spiritual direction is, as we have seen, the person's experience of God. The engine that drives spiritual direction is not a curriculum that needs to be taught but the call of Spirit to spirit—what I have been calling spiritual longing. And the true teacher is the Holy Spirit, not the spiritual director.

While there were elements of teaching in these brief encounters, I would describe my role as more like that of a tutor or coach. I listened, I encouraged, I made a couple of suggestions, and most important, I attempted to turn our dialogue into prayer. This means that I attempted to make it a dialogue of three persons, not two. By asking for attentiveness to the presence of God in the moment, I was encouraging prayer. Whether we closed our eyes and offered formal worded prayers or not, we were in prayer. And our focus was Bill's experience of God.

I noted earlier that spiritual direction is not authoritarian. This does not mean, however, that it may not at times be directive. In this example I was fairly directive with Bill. I asked him questions, and repeatedly I directed his attention to the Spirit. I also suggested things he might consider doing. I was not, however, functioning as an authority figure. Nor did he ever experience me as such.

One final aspect of my work with Bill worth noting is the way I handled his question about my own spiritual journey. If spiritual directors had to be spiritual giants, they would need to avoid sharing any moments of struggle or inadequacy. But spiritual guides are simply fellow pilgrims on the journey who are willing to be honest about their own struggles and successes and who know how to do so without taking the focus off either God or the person they are seeking to help.

Counselors and teachers generally avoid self-disclosure. Spiritual directors are willing to share themselves and their story. However, they should never lose sight of the fact that the true spiritual director is the Spirit of God. This keeps them from focusing either their own attention or the attention of the person who has sought their help on themselves.

Attending to God's Communication

Central to my work with Bill was an attempt to foster the deepening of his relationship to God. Communication is foundational to any relationship. This is why prayer is central both to the Christian spiritual journey and to relationships of spiritual direction.

Communication and revelation are foundational to the character of God. A time of apparent silence may be experienced as a "dark night of the soul," but when we can affirm that God is still present, we can follow his lead to deeper places of growth and intimacy with him. His presence is often a hidden one because we look for him in the wrong places. The One who promises to be with us always to the end of all times (Matthew 28:20) may be with us in ways we fail to notice. Who does not regularly fail to perceive him in the hungry, thirsty strangers and those in need? Who does not fail to meet him in Scripture when, on reading, we encounter words rather than the

Word? Spiritual direction seeks to help us attune ourselves to God's communication to us. Attentiveness to this communication is foundational to spiritual growth.

The rich notion of "a relationship with God" means many things. At a most basic level, whether we realize it or not, all humans are in relation to the God who created them and who seeks them in redemptive love. We are not in relationship to God merely when we are conscious of such a relationship. As creatures of a Creator God, we stand in relationship to him whether we ignore him, protest his unreality or surrender to his loving will and Spirit.

But when we talk about deepening a relationship with God, we usually refer to the personal relationship that, almost unbelievably, we affirm he desires with us. This personal nature of the relationship brings prayer back into focus. There is no such thing as a relationship apart from communication. Communication with God is prayer. Prayer is the heart of our relationship with God. And prayer is the core of spiritual direction.

Reflecting on the Nature of Spiritual Direction
It is my hope that this chapter has reduced some of the mystery about spiritual direction. While the term may still be somewhat unfamiliar, the relationship it describes is not as dissimilar to other relationships of spiritual nurture as it may appear. It differs from preaching, counseling, moral guidance and relationships of discipling or shepherding in emphasis, not in absolute terms.

However, while it shares important features with other relationships of spiritual support, one crucial difference is the centrality of prayer in spiritual direction. Spiritual direction is prayer because it is a conversation not simply between two people but between two people and God. Attentiveness to God's presence and to one's experience of that presence are at the very core of spiritual direction. This, not the director's advice about how to live the Christian life, is the engine that drives the transformational journey in spiritual direction.

Focusing on spiritual experience does not mean talking only about spiritual matters. While the goal is discerning the presence and leading of the Spirit of God and surrendering to his will, spiritual experience occurs within the midst of daily experience. It is here that we must discern the presence of God if we are to move closer toward prayer without ceasing. And it is here that spiritual direction begins its attempt to help us discern the presence of God in the midst of life.

❊ Reflect on conversations and relationships that have increased your attentiveness to the presence and leading of the Spirit. As you review them, identify what you can learn from them about giving this same gift to others. Ask God to guide you in this, and thank him for the people he has brought into your life to serve in this capacity.

Attending to God's presence with us is prayer. Prayer is not simply talking. It also includes listening, gazing, meditating and any act of attending to God. Prayer without ceasing would be impossible if we had to be talking to him all day long. It becomes more possible as we begin to allow our consciousness to be transformed by attending to the presence of God.

❊ Reflect on your experience of God in prayer. What makes it hard for you to engage in prayer as attentive listening to God as opposed to simply talking to him? How aware of his presence are you throughout the day? What might you be able to do to increase your God consciousness? Journal on these reflections, and look for an opportunity to discuss them with someone.

5

Soul
Attunement

*T*he question I am asked most often by people interested in becoming spiritual directors is "What exactly do spiritual directors do?" The simple and most direct answer I can give is that they help others attend to God's presence and revelation and prepare to respond to him. In other words, they help people attune themselves to God.

Attending

The attunement of our self to God is not a simple matter. Aligning ourselves with God to be more aware of his presence and receptive to his will is central to the task of Christian spiritual formation. It is a lifelong process. No one gets past the need—as described by Brother Lawrence—to practice the presence of God. Spiritual direction is a relationship devoted to the practice of this spiritual discipline.

People who seek out a spiritual director are generally not neophytes in the Christian spiritual journey. Usually they have already made significant progress in following Christ and in the life of faith. They have begun to learn to discern God's presence in their lives and often have a well-developed prayer life.

Typically what they want from spiritual direction is a deepening of these spiritual disciplines. They want a keener sense of God's presence with them. And they want help in deepening their relationship with him. The master goal of spiritual direction can therefore be described as *the facilitation of this attunement to God's presence.*

The notion of tuning ourselves to God reminds us that he is constantly communicating with us. His Word, his creation, his Spirit all continually pour out his revelation. Our job is to increase our sensitivity to that communication. As a radio receiver is tuned to receive transmissions on a certain frequency, so our souls can be tuned to be open maximally to the communications of a God who constantly reaches out to us in revelation.

God's very nature is revelation. He did not simply reveal himself at some point in the past. God has no more ceased being revelation than he has ceased being love. Revelation is his nature. Christian spirituality grows out of the attunement of our souls to the revealing God who seeks us out and calls us to know him and his love.

Relationships develop only when people pay attention to each other. When self-absorption blocks attentiveness to the other person, relationships are impoverished. Our relationship with the Lord depends on our attentiveness to him. Learning to be attuned to God lies thus at the very core of spiritual direction. Spiritual directors facilitate attunement to God by encouraging those who seek their help to attend to six things:

- ❊ their experience of God
- ❊ Jesus
- ❊ God's presence with them
- ❊ God's attention to them
- ❊ God's revelation through Scripture
- ❊ God's revelation through their dreams

Let us examine each of these.

Attending to one's experience of God. When people begin a relationship of spiritual direction, they often ask what they should talk about. My answer is their experience of God.

Spiritual direction is not the best place to discuss one's symptoms, one's theology or one's church and its frustrations. It is, however, an excellent place to discuss the ways one experiences God.

Some people have great difficulty moving from their ideas of God to their experience. Listen in on part of a conversation with Larry and his spiritual director (SD) to see one way to help such a person.

SD: You have been telling me about what you want from God. But tell me a bit more about how you actually experience him.

Larry: Well, I know God is love, and I know I can trust him. Is that what you mean?

SD: I hear you making a theological assertion. But how do you experience God's love? Or how do you experience his trustworthiness?

Larry: I'm not sure what you mean. I just believe that Jesus loves me. That's what I have always been taught, and I do believe it.

SD: That's important. I'm glad you believe it, because it is true. But if you only had your direct personal experience of God to rely on, what would you tell me about this God you believe exists?

Larry: I guess I'd say I experience his forgiveness of my sins. Is that what you mean?

SD: Yes. Tell me more about that.

Larry: Well, when I pray for forgiveness, generally I feel forgiven. I feel guilt when I sin and relief after I pray for forgiveness.

SD: Great. When else do you know from experience that God is in direct contact with you?

Larry: Sometimes in worship services.

SD: Tell me more about that.

The biblical pattern of faith suggests that personal experience of God plays an important foundation in Christ following. Beliefs about God are to flow out of experience, not simply to be given intellectual assent. Someone simply believing that God is love does not honor him. He wants us to know that love personally. He wants us to surrender to his love, not merely to beliefs and obligations.

Spiritual direction facilitates attunement to God when it encourages interior reflection on personal experience of God. Far from being merely some psychological technique, this is a spiritual discipline that is foundational to knowing God genuinely. Spiritual experience is experience of God. Without this there is little headway made on the spiritual journey.

Attending to Jesus. Christian spirituality is grounded in Jesus. Paul tells us that in Jesus is the fullness of the Godhead revealed (Colossians 2:9). Jesus was God incarnate. Christian spirituality is not therefore merely built on a foundation of knowing God but necessarily involves knowing God as revealed in Jesus. Attending to Jesus is a foundational part of attuning our souls to God.

In his engaging and eminently wise little book *Christ-Following*[1] Trevor Hudson urges filtering all our ideas about God through the decisive disclosure of himself in Jesus of Nazareth. Every idea and assumption we have about God must be measured against the person of Jesus. For most of us, this will give us an opportunity to redraw our image of God. This is one of the most important ways in which Christian spirituality matures—by allowing immature and incorrect ideas of God to be reformed. The filter for that reformation is, as Hudson reminds us, Jesus of Nazareth.

Meditation on the Gospel accounts of Jesus' life has been the core of many Roman Catholic approaches to spiritual formation. We Protestants do well to learn from them in this regard. Bible reading can take many forms. Nonmeditative reading may involve

---

[1]Trevor Hudson, *Christ-Following: Ten Signposts to Spirituality* (Grand Rapids, Mich.: Revell, 1996).

some reflection, but it is usually more oriented toward analysis and comprehension of content. For years I read the Bible this way, attempting to discover or be reminded of things that would help me live the Christian life.

Meditative reading is less focused on the words and more focused on the Word behind the words. In the case of meditation on Gospel accounts of Jesus, the intent is to come to know Jesus better. This involves lingering over the story long enough to allow yourself to meet Jesus in the account. It involves daydreaming on what you read, not attempting to analyze it or even learn from it.

Imagination necessarily plays a part in this engagement. This makes some people nervous. Often this is based on a naive assumption that God's revelation of himself can be received in some manner that bypasses the subjectivity of our experience. It cannot. God wants to meet us in our depths, and the imaginative, intuitive and subjective parts of our self must be part of that encounter if it is to be genuine.

No one has anything to fear about imagination that is guided by meditation on Scripture and the Spirit of God. This can take many forms. Any moment in the life of Christ or any of his teachings or parables offers rich opportunities for meeting Jesus. Consider this fragment of a conversation with a woman named Angie with whom I worked in spiritual direction.

Angie struggled in her Christ following. Her personal history made her deeply uncomfortable in the church—any church—and her relationship to Christians was filled with ambivalence. However, her spiritual yearning was fervent, and she entered spiritual direction out of a longing to encounter God more deeply.

After we explored the contours of her spiritual journey, I asked her about her experience of God. She told me how much trouble she had relating to Christ. Her perceptions of him were all tainted by dysfunctional childhood family and church experiences. I then asked about her ability to meet Christ in church or in Scripture. She said that she was sometimes deeply aware of meeting him in the liturgy but that the Bible tended to leave her cold, as it had been used more as a weapon than an instrument of grace in her childhood.

I asked if she was willing to risk meeting the Jesus of the Gospels. She said she was. I prayed with her, asking that she would be enabled to meet the Jesus who truly incarnated the fullness of the Godhead, not the Jesus of her personal history. We then read together a single verse of Scripture—Matthew 19:14, where Jesus tells the disciples to let the little children come to him. I encouraged her to sit quietly before this scene of children thronging to Jesus as he opened his arms and encouraged them to come, sit on his knee and look into his face. I suggested that she do the same.

Angie sat very quietly for several moments, deep in thought with her eyes shut. Slowly she began to cry. I did not interrupt the experience. After a few moments she said, "Is that really true? Does he really want the little wounded girl that is in me to come and sit on his lap? Can that really be true?"

"It can, and it is," I said. "Just stay with that image and listen to Jesus' words to you—'Let the little children alone, and do not stop them coming to me, for it is to such as these that the kingdom of heaven belongs.' Look at him and listen to him. He is speaking to you."

Angie continued to sob quietly, her head hung low with her hands over her face. After a few moments she sat up straight, slowly smiling, and gradually put words to her experience.

"If that really is Jesus, then I have no trouble coming to him at all. The Jesus I have usually encountered is not at all like him. He is harsh, judgmental, condemning—much like people in the church where I grew up. Can I really trust that this is the true Jesus?"

"You can," I said. "And the reason is that he is the Jesus of the Gospels. Take some time this next couple of weeks before we meet again and see what else you can learn about him." I then gave her several additional passages for similar meditation—John 6:35-40 (Jesus the Bread of Life) and John 7:37-38 (Jesus the Source of Living Water).

Angie had been on the journey of Christian spirituality for a long time. However, her progress was seriously limited by her unfamiliarity with the Jesus of the Gospels. Her ideas of God needed reformation in the light of the decisive revelation of God in Christ. She needed to get to know Jesus better. Helping her pay attention to the Jesus of the Gospels played a crucially important role in helping her spiritual journey.

The only way to come to know Jesus is through the Gospels. There is no substitute for meditation on Scripture as a route to a deep, personal engagement with God. Attunement to the Christian God must always involve attending to Jesus.

Attending to God's presence. The writings of St. Ignatius, particularly his *Spiritual Exercises,* offer enormous help to those seeking to provide spiritual direction to others. Probably the most valuable of the many gifts I have received from the Ignatian approach to spiritual formation is its concept of the examination of consciousness—or as it is usually described, the examen. I illustrated it in the last chapter as part of the discussion of my work with Bill. I did not, however, name it.

The examen is a time of prayerful reflection on one's experience of the presence of God over recent hours. The reason it is called an examination of consciousness is that its goal is the transformation of consciousness by increasing awareness of God's presence. If attentiveness to God's presence is prayer, the examen is a discipline that moves us closer toward the goal of prayer without ceasing. When blessed by God, this discipline holds the possibility of transforming our experience—both conscious and unconscious.

As usually undertaken, the examen is done at the end of each day. I begin by imagining myself in the presence of Jesus. In dialogue with Jesus, I thank him for the day and his presence during it. Praying for the guidance of the Holy Spirit, I then ask for the grace to see the day as God sees it. This is often best done by imagining myself watching the day with Jesus, letting it float by as from a moving train or a fast-forwarded VCR. The instruction is to let

Jesus stop the train (or the VCR), allowing him to interrupt the stream of consciousness and focus on whatever parts of the day warrant reflection.

Doing this, I find fragments of my day coming to mind. As they do, the goal is to notice how aware I was of God's presence in each experience. How conscious of God was I at that moment? If I was not aware of his presence, what was blocking that awareness? If God seemed absent, can I now discern his presence? This then should be followed by sorrowful repentance for failures to see God and gratitude for times of awareness of him. Finally, I end with a prayer for help in being more aware of his presence during the next day, and I journal any discoveries made during the examen.

Like any spiritual discipline, this simple exercise can be demanding. Although it should not take longer than fifteen minutes, for the beginner it can easily be fifteen minutes of struggle with concentration. If this occurs, do not struggle but follow each period of wandering attention with a gentle repetition of a prayer that Jesus would control what thoughts about the day come to mind. Believe, then, that whatever comes to mind about the day is what you should examine.

When Carla first began to practice a daily examen, she was immediately struck by how much of the time she was in fact already conscious of God's presence. Her nightly examen provided a wonderful opportunity for an expression of gratitude. However, she also came to see that God was present with her in times and ways that she had been failing to note. Her daily review began to help her identify a hidden Christ in encounters with people where theologically she had not expected to find him. He also turned up in experiences that were far from obviously religious or spiritual but within which she could discern his providence, grace and love.

Justin found the exercise difficult. Although he had a well-developed prayer life, it was primarily built on discipline rather than surrender. He found it difficult to let go of his thoughts and allow Jesus to direct his attention. That in itself was instructive for him. Over time, however, he got better at taking his hands off the controls. Slowly this taught him not only to attend better to God's presence but to surrender to God's Spirit.

Attending to God's presence is prayer. Increasing one's attunement to the ever-present God is living a life of prayer. Worded prayers form part of such a life. But prayer is much more than worded prayers. An increased sense of God's presence is the blessing of prayer that does not originate with me but is a direct and personal gift of the God whose name is Revelation. Attending to God's presence allows prayer to emerge from within me, not simply to be a disciplined offering of words at those times when I remember to pray.

Attending to God's attention to you. When I am away from home and my wife is not with me, I am comforted by the thought that she is thinking of me and missing me. First thing in the morning I know she will be praying for me. Last thing at night I know I will again be in her thoughts and prayers. It is like this with God. And attending to his attention to me is an excellent way to increase my awareness of his presence.

Psalm 5:3 describes this interaction of God's attentiveness to us and our attentiveness to him. The Jerusalem Bible offers a particularly wonderful translation of this passage:

> I say this prayer to you, Yahweh,
>   for at daybreak you listen for my voice;
> and at dawn I hold myself in readiness for you,
>   I watch for you.

What an extraordinary image—God eagerly waiting for me at daybreak, listening for my voice! If I go to bed meditating on this truth, how can I awake with anything other than the expectation described by the psalmist—eagerly holding myself in readiness for the God who eagerly holds himself in readiness for me?

Scripture is full of such images of God watching over us, hearing our cries and feeling our pain. The psalms are particularly rich in this regard, providing many excellent passages for meditation on God's attentiveness to us. Another of my favorites is Psalm 121—a psalm that describes God's inexhaustible watchfulness over us. The God I am trying to orient my attention to is a God whose attention is continually on me. He never sleeps, nor does he even get tired! He watches over me twenty-four hours a day, 365 days a year, now and forevermore! My attention to him is not needed to make him take note of me. It is merely a way of increasing consciousness of his loving, constant attention to me.

Attending to God's revelation through Scripture. In the discussions of meditating on Jesus and on God's attention to us I have already pointed to the importance of attending to God's revelation in Scripture. But God can also be met in the rest of the Scripture, and attentiveness to this revelation forms an important part of attunement of one's soul to God.

Most people who seek out spiritual direction already have regular exposure to Scripture through some combination of personal reading and corporate worship. Some, however, need to be encouraged to increase personal reading of the Bible. The goal of doing so in spiritual direction is not simply doctrinal instruction or correction but meeting God. Let's explore this by returning to the story of Angie.

For some time after the session I recounted earlier, Angie continued to focus on Jesus, seeking to encounter him through the Gospels. Increasingly, however, she came to speak of the great difference between Jesus and the God of the Old Testament. It seemed important therefore for her to meet God the Father of Jesus as he revealed himself in the rest of Scripture. Again, the goal was not simply to teach some point of theology. It was to facilitate her attunement to God.

I first did this by encouraging her to read and meditate on the Genesis account of the creation and fall of humans. My instruction was for her to watch for the hidden presence of Jesus—the God of grace she had come to meet in the Gospels. Praying for eyes to discern grace, she went off to read and meditate on the first three chapters of Genesis.

She returned to our next meeting with considerable excitement. Something totally new had struck her. She was deeply impressed by the care God took to prepare garments of skin for Adam and Eve after they discovered their nakedness and were overwhelmed with their shame. She added, "Had God been like I have often pictured him, he would have wanted to rub their noses in their shame to make sure they learned their lesson. I was so impressed that what he seemed to want was to eliminate their shame, not exploit it." This was a profound insight for her. It led to a cascading series of subsequent insights about the nature of God as she subsequently meditated on other Old Testament passages.

Scripture is given for our instruction and edification. In its totality Scripture presents the God revealed in Jesus and whom we seek to follow. The story of his pursuit of humankind despite our unfaithfulness is a story of grace. Biblical revelation aids our attunement to God by helping us encounter the Lord God of heaven and earth, not simply the god of our imagination, childhood experience or previous religious instruction.

Attending to God's revelation through dreams. Dreams may seem like a strange place to seek God's presence, but in fact they can be a rich resource for increasing attunement to him. As I have written on this extensively elsewhere,[2] I will be brief on the matter here. During the twenty years I have been regularly attending to my dreams, this has been a singularly productive way of meeting God in my depths. Thus it is also a powerful resource for the attunement of the soul to God.

Dreams provide us with an opportunity to know what Daniel called our "inmost thoughts" (Daniel 2:30). This summarizes the essential understanding of dreams offered by modern depth psy-

---

[2]David G. Benner, *Care of Souls: Revisioning Christian Nurture and Counsel* (Grand Rapids, Mich.: Baker, 1998).

chology. It is also the basis of the enormous spiritual potential of dreams.

Dreams are most useful in spiritual growth when we prayerfully listen to them rather than seek to interpret them. We should receive them as gifts from God, asking him what he wishes to draw to our attention through them.

Attending to dreams begins when you place a journal by your bed so that any dream can be recorded immediately after waking. Once the details of the dream are recorded, further dream work can be undertaken whenever is most suitable. If, however, the dream is not recorded immediately when you wake, it will not be available for reflection when you are ready to turn to it.

The most basic dream work exercise can be summarized under the mnemonic TTAQ.[3] This points to four exercises that should be done to attend to a dream that seems potentially significant.

T Title—give the dream a title

T Theme—note its overall theme

A Affect—note the dominant emotions in the dream and now as you prayerfully reflect on it

Q Question—note the potential questions the dream poses for you

Bill, the pastor introduced in the previous chapter, had never done any dream work but expressed interest in it after reading my book. He reported that his dreams seemed to be infrequent and that when he could remember them, they generally seemed to be a simple rehashing of the events of his day. He asked where he should start.

I suggested that he tell God that he would be listening if God wished to communicate with him through his dreams. I also suggested that he ask for help in remembering important dreams and discernment in hearing what God was saying through them. He did this. A few days later he had the following dream.

---

[3]Louis M. Savary et al., *Dreams and Spiritual Growth* (New York: Paulist, 1984).

I dreamt that I was walking through the streets of a busy city, filled with noise and people. The scene seemed familiar, although I didn't know where it was. It was a hot, humid summer day. I was sweating and my feet hurt. I didn't know where I was going, but I had a sense of being late. Suddenly I noticed that I was beside a tall stone wall. I was surprised because I had never seen this wall before. I wondered what was behind it, suspecting it to be an embassy or some important residence. My interest in it increased as I continued to walk up the street. When I finally reached a gate, I was disappointed to see that it was locked. Looking through the gate, I could see a wonderful garden. I wondered whose it was. I noticed how cool it looked. I wanted to enter it and sit beneath one of the trees. I recall thinking I would be late for wherever I was rushing to get, but I didn't care; I just wanted to rest in that garden. And then I awoke.

He then shared with me his basic work with the TTAQ technique.

Title: The Garden Calls
Theme: Longing for stillness of soul
Affect: Surprise, longing, release
Questions: 1. What is the garden God is inviting me to enter?
         2. Why have I not noticed the garden before?

I asked him what spiritual insights he had received from prayerful reflection on these questions.

Bill: I'm really glad you encouraged me not to attempt to analyze the dream. That was hard to resist, although I have no idea where I would go with it. I did, however, keep wondering why I had never noticed the garden, since the street seemed so familiar.

David: But as you prayed about the questions, did you receive any gifts from God, any insights around the questions you identified?

Bill: I'm not sure. What I did find was an increased longing for the garden. It's strange how that image stayed with me. It's like someone inside it was calling to me, inviting me to enter. But I don't know how to do that. And I had the sense that it wasn't my garden, that I didn't belong in it.

David: Let's just assume for a moment that it may have been God calling to you, inviting you to enter some special place where he wants to meet you. What might such a call mean?

Bill: I wondered about that, but it seemed to be reading too much into it. Maybe it's just a reflection of my need for rest.

David: But let me return to my question. If this dream was an answer to your prayer that God meet you in your sleep, what might he be saying to you?

Bill: Maybe he is telling me he wants to meet me in that garden, in a place of quiet.

David: Maybe he is telling you that he is looking forward to spending time with you in your soul garden, the place you are beginning to cultivate as you seek to nurture your inner self, not just your outer self.

Bill: I agree. I find that encouraging. That's why I am here. That's what I want more than anything else.

Not all of Bill's dreams yielded such easily picked spiritual fruit. Nor did dream work ever become a major part of his work in spiritual direction. However, by means of occasional dreams he found himself freshly appreciating the way God could communicate with him in his depths. And in so doing, he allowed the Spirit of God to increasingly attune him in his depths.

Responding

Besides helping others attune themselves to God's presence and revelation, spiritual directors are to help directees prepare to respond to God's call.

Some people tend to think of God's call as simply a call to conversion. Others think of it as a vocational matter, often particularly a calling to a religious vocation. Both understandings seriously limit the nature of God's call. God continuously reaches out to humans. His call is always the same. It is an invitation to come to him, to receive his rest, enjoy his love and respond with obedient service that flows out of devotion. Our response is also the same at all points of the spiritual journey. The response he seeks is surrender to his love.

Obedience is a poor substitute for surrender to love. Those who love obey. But not all obedience is motivated by love. Too easily we offer God obedience that is not a heart response, merely a behavioral one. Too easily fear, guilt or a desire to manipulate God can motivate obedience.

I may obey God solely because I fear not doing so. I may fear his judgment. Or I may fear the censure of others. Fear is always an inadequate foundation for genuinely Christian spirituality.

Or I may obey God out of guilt. I may feel that if I obey him in the present, I can somehow atone for not having done so in the past. Such self-justification is but one of the many subtle forms of the works righteousness that seems programmed into the human soul.

Finally, I may obey God so he will look favorably on my petitions and me. This is but a thin Christian veneer on the basic pre-Christian desire of humans to appease the gods whatever it takes. It has no place in genuine Christianity.

What God desires is surrender to his love. God is love. To know him genuinely is to love him. And those we love we seek to serve. Service born out of devotion may superficially look like service offered out of obligation, but it is fueled by a wholly different dynamic. Obedient service offered out of love is a response to a lover, not a response to an authority figure. As noted previously, genuine Christian obedience is always much more like the response of lovers to each other than that of slaves to masters.

The spiritual-direction experience of Bill shows how this can work out in the experience of someone who is already well established on the Christian spiritual journey.

Bill knew lots about obedience but not so much about surrender to love. I do not mean to suggest that his obedience was all merely motivated by fear or guilt or a desire to manipulate God. He genuinely wanted to serve God, and his life had long been oriented to this cardinal desire. However, he had much to learn about the depths of God's personal love for him and much transformation to undergo as he allowed his response to this love to be the source of everything he did.

At one point as we were exploring this question, Bill voiced a fear about making devotion to God the source of his motivation for service: if this were to be the case, he might not work as hard as he currently did. Even saying this was an insight to him. As we explored this feeling, Bill's desire for a deepened life of devotion was even further intensified.

Around this time Bill began one of his sessions by telling me about a book on contemplative prayer that he was reading. We talked about this book for a few moments, until I asked him how the ideas we were discussing related to his own prayer life. I did this to ensure that our focus was on his spiritual experience, not his ideas.

He told me that his daily Bible reading had recently been Luke 10:38-42, the story of Jesus in the home of Mary and Martha. What had struck him in meditating on this story was how much he wanted to move from being a Martha—always active in doing things to serve Jesus—to being more like Mary, sitting quietly at Jesus' feet, gazing on him. He had had this thought on previous occasions, and it was in fact part of his motivation to undertake the retreat where we had met. "However," Bill said, "I was reminded the last time we were together just how uncomfortable I am simply being in God's presence and not filling the space between us with words. I want to learn to pray contemplatively."

"What does that mean to you?" I asked.

"What I think it means is prayer that comes more from my heart than my head. I guess it also means prayer that is less built around words than attentiveness to presence. What I want to learn to do is be still before God and enjoy his presence. I really want to learn to be like Mary, simply sitting at the feet of Jesus and gazing on him. If I do that, I am quite convinced that when I am not sitting at his feet, my service will be motivated by that same devotion."

"Why don't we take some time right now to allow you to do just that? Simply shut your eyes and enjoy the presence of the Lord. Look at him as he gazes back at you with his full loving attention and asks you to sit with him for a while. Tell me where that leads you."

Bill was silent for several moments. Finally he spoke.

"What Jesus seems to be saying to me is that what he wants of me is less related to what I do than who I am. As I look at him in my mind, I remember his words in Scripture that assure me of how deeply he loves me. I really am moved by that love. I do want to release my striving to do things for him to the purification of his love. I do want to allow his love to refine my obedience and service."

Bill was not new at the business of loving God. But we all need reminders that what God primarily wants is our love and friendship. We also need reminders that the knowing of God that he invites is primarily a knowing through love. How often we substitute *knowing about* for genuine *knowing*. Heart knowing (knowing through love) is compatible with head knowing (knowing about). But when our knowing of God begins with heart knowing, the head knowing that follows will be based on personal experience, not merely intellectual assent.

Again, the samples of spiritual direction offered in this chapter should be understood as illustrations, not models. I am far from a master spiritual director. My work with others is also constrained by the limitations of my own knowing of God's love and response to it. But as I am able to align myself with the Holy Spirit—the true spiritual director—I am blessed by being able to be a part of others' spiritual journeys toward increasing intimacy with God and the life of devotion and surrender that flows out of such intimacy.

Reflecting on Soul Attunement

Attunement to God's presence and revelation lies at the very core of Christian spiritual formation. For this reason it also lies at the core of spiritual direction. Spiritual directors help others attend to God and prepare to respond to what they encounter.

Many people find that attending to God is greatly aided by meditating on his watchfulness over us.

■ Read Psalm 121 slowly and meditatively. Allow yourself to daydream on the inexhaustible watchfulness of God. Note your experience in your journal.

The daily examen is another discipline that many people find helpful in learning to discern the presence of God in everyday experience.

■ Review the discussion of the daily examen in this chapter. Consider following this discipline for two weeks. If you do, find someone with whom you can discuss your experience.

Attending to God should also include attending to Jesus as he is revealed in the Gospels, and to God as he is revealed throughout the rest of Scripture. This should not be reduced to simply reading or studying the Bible. The goal should be to come to know the Word behind the words.

■ How well do you know the Jesus of the Gospels? Do you need fresh ways to approach God through Scripture?

Dreams can be aids to spiritual growth. Although this should never be the primary place we seek to discern God's presence, prayerful attention to dreams can help us know our innermost thoughts. Because the transformational journey must start on the inside, not the outside, meeting God in our depths and allowing him access to our innermost world is a crucial part of Christian spirituality. Attending to dreams does not have to form a part of this. However, it can, and countless Christians across the ages have witnessed the unique potential of dreams in the process of spiritual transformation.

◉ After reading this chapter, what potential spiritual value do you see in dreams? If you have never attended to your own dreams, consider establishing a dream journal and doing so. If you do, find someone with whom you can share your discoveries and questions—someone you can spiritually trust regardless of his or her expertise in dream work.

Finally, soul attunement involves not just attending but also responding to God's call. This call is always a call of love, and the response God desires is surrender. While the concept of surrender to anything may have frightening connotations to some people, surrender to perfect love should not arouse fear. This should be the foundation of the Christian life—surrender to love as the motive for obedience and service.

◉ How might your response to God be different if utter certainty that you are deeply loved by God were the foundation of your identity? What keeps you from a more complete surrender to God's love? What currently motivates your obedience and service?

6

A Portrait
of the Process

*P*revious chapters have included a number of fragments of spiritual direction dialogue. To better illustrate the way a spiritual direction relationship unfolds, this chapter presents an extended illustration.

Su Yin is a Chinese Christian living in a major city in Southeast Asia. Initially trained as a physician, she subsequently returned to seminary, was ordained and has for several years been serving as pastor of a growing evangelical church. I first met her when she attended a series of lectures I gave in her city. We spoke on several occasions over the course of these days, and she subsequently contacted me, asking if I would be willing to offer her spiritual direction by e-mail.

E-mail generally is not the preferred medium for spiritual direction. Because of the absence of nonverbal contextual cues, it forces reliance on the explicit and verbal dimensions of dialogue. It also leaves communication more open to misunderstanding. Yet I have often been surprised at how effective it can be. Sometimes it is the only way people can receive the help they desire. And some people come to feel that the advantages of being able to write whenever they have something to share and read the reply whenever is most convenient for them vastly outweigh any minor disadvantages.

What follows is a synopsis of my e-mail interaction with Su Yin as it unfolded over the course of approximately two years. Generally her messages came about once a week, with occasional intervals of two or three weeks. I began by suggesting that she tell me something of her present experience of God, as well as what she wanted from him. I also asked what she wanted from me. This got us immediately under way.

> Dear Dr. Benner (or may I call you David?):
> You asked about my experience of God and what I want from him. Although I am quick to say that nothing is more important to me than my relationship with God, I am increasingly aware that I don't know him as deeply as I desire. I speak to him more than with him and am better at speaking than listening to him. I often think of myself as like the older brother of the prodigal son. I have stayed close to the Father, and it would be easy to assume that because I have never left his house, I know him well. But watching the return of my younger brother, I realize that I have never experienced the Father's love in the way he has. As I listened to your lectures, I also realize how much my knowing of God is a head, not a heart, knowing. I know a great deal about God, but at times I wonder how much I actually know him in experience. I long to really know his love and to love him deeply in return. I long to learn to spend time with him, not simply talking at him but talking with him. These are my deepest desires.
>
> What I want from spiritual direction is someone to share my spiritual journey with. It's often lonely as the pastor of a church. Everyone expects me to be spiritually strong, to have all the answers. I know better than to ask this of you. All I really want is the opportunity to share matters of my soul with you. I am sure I will also have questions as we proceed, but I am not looking for you to tell me what

to do, only to discuss my questions with me. Does this sound reasonable?

Yours in Christ,

Su Yin

Dear Su Yin:

Please do call me David. This is much too personal a relationship for titles to get in the way. I hear your longings and will make them my prayer for you. It is a prayer that God will answer. Your longings are from God. Your expectations of me, and of the spiritual direction experience, seem reasonable.

Please tell me more about your experience of God in prayer. I think we will find that this will lead us to the places you need to go in seeking deeper intimacy with the Lord.

David

Dear David:

Thank you for your prayers for me. Let me tell you more about my own prayer life.

As you may have recognized in our brief face-to-face conversations, I am a disciplined person. Discipline served me well in my studies, and it has served me well in my ministry. However, I sometimes wonder if its effect on my prayer life is not more mixed.

I rise early each morning and spend a half-hour in devotional Scripture reading and half an hour in prayer. My prayer time combines a response to my reading, thanksgiving for current blessings and petitions for a list of people for whom I pray. I do this almost every day of the year, whether I feel like it or not. It is an exercise of discipline—done because I know it is what I should do, regardless of my experience. I have been taught (and now teach others) that we shouldn't look to our experience to confirm truths that we believe in our hearts. Do you agree? Your emphasis on personal experience of God is a little unsettling to me in this regard. However, I don't want to be a slave to discipline. In fact, after listening to you speak when you were here, I wonder if my spiritual life is based more on discipline than devotion. That is something I'd like to explore further.

Rereading your last message, I see that I haven't answered your question about my experience of God in prayer. Perhaps it is significant that I spoke instead about my patterns of prayer and ignored the question of my experience. I am embarrassed to admit this, but I have to say I don't have much experience of God in prayer. I pray and I trust he is there listening. But, as I said in the last message, I view prayer more as talking than listening or conversation. I do the talking and that pretty much fills up the time and my experience.

I'm not sure where to go with this. My questions about experience aside, I do want to be more aware of God's presence—in prayer and during the course of my day. I feel that something is lacking but am not sure what to do next. Do you have any suggestions?
Su Yin

Dear Su Yin:
Spiritual disciplines serve us well and should never be despised. However, you are correct in suspecting that they can be a substitute (and a poor one at that) for an ever-deepening personal relationship with God.

Allow your answer to the question of what place personal experience of God is to play in Christian spirituality to come from a meditation on the Gospel account of the development of faith in the disciples of Jesus. As you have time, study and reflect on this question and let me know what you discover.

In response to your request for help in increasing your awareness of God's presence, I wonder if you would like to try something that many people find to be a helpful way of doing this. [Here I introduced the examen described in the previous chapter and asked her if it was something she wanted to try.]
David

Dear David:
I undertook the study you suggested and found some surprising things. The disciples seemed to initially make a response of faith to a call that they could not have fully understood. Their faith must have been initially based on quite limited personal experience. However, over time, their experience of God seemed to mature their faith. Their growing belief that he was the Messiah was based on their experience of him. In

him, they encountered the Christ. This was the basis of their conviction. Experience did seem to play a role.

Perhaps rather than seek an answer to my question, I am ready now to restate it. Perhaps my more fundamental question is how I can experience God more deeply. How can I know him in a way that will inform and support my beliefs about him?

My first experiences with the examen produced a similarly surprising result. What I discovered is that although I spend my day thinking and talking about God, I am actually not conscious of his presence as much as I'd like to be. My prayer has become "Open mine eyes that I may see you." I will keep you posted on further results.

Su Yin

Over the course of these first few interchanges, a rhythm of interacting has begun to evolve. While sometimes e-mail spiritual direction takes the form of long but infrequent messages, Su Yin was using the relationship to deal with smaller chunks of experience. When this suits the person and circumstances, it often tends to work better.

Notice how I have encouraged her to dialogue not simply with me but with God. I did this by encouraging her to seek answers to questions in Scripture and by the practice of the daily examen, a time of daily prayer. Beyond the regular value that this holds for anyone, my hope was that it might speak to her desire to begin to develop a prayer life that included listening, not simply talking.

The other reason I turned her question back to Scripture is that I did not want her to set me up as an authority figure who would answer her questions. This does not mean I would avoid answering every question she asked. But I was attempting to establish a three-way dialogue (between her, God and me), not simply a student-teacher relationship in which she would ask questions and I would answer them.

Let us pick up the interaction with Su Yin after a few intervening e-mails, when she returns to some discussion about her experience in the examen.

Dear David:

I have now been doing a daily examen for a little over a month and want to share with you how it is going. I have been receiving some wonderful blessings through this exercise. Many nights I still find that I passed through the day with little awareness of his presence. But increasingly, I end the day with a clear sense that God was with me during it. I am also experiencing real joy and gratitude in this awareness.

What I now want is more of my day to be filled with prayer. I long to have an ongoing conversation with God. How sad I feel when I discover that hours or even a whole day has gone by and I haven't even thought of him once. I still seem a long, long way from "ceaseless prayer." Do you have any suggestions about what I should be doing next?
Su Yin

Dear Su Yin:

God appears to be beginning to answer your prayer for an increased sense of his presence. I thank him with you for this. What is prayer if it is not an attunement to his presence? How do you wish to respond to that presence? That too is prayer.
David

Dear David:

Your comment about prayer makes me realize that I have indeed been praying. My heart has been increasingly filled with gratitude for the growing sense of the presence of God that I experience. I accept this as prayer.

This discovery is having a surprising and somewhat disturbing effect. It makes me wonder about my discipline of worded prayer. Is it any less prayer? Is it still important? It feels more mechanical as I am beginning to look to God and speak with him throughout my day. Can these two forms of prayer be brought together? Should they be integrated? Is one of more value than the other? Any suggestions or comments?
Su Yin

This e-mail made me pause. It made me think of my own experience in prayer. For many years my prayer life had been simply an expression of discipline. Then frustration with the limited fruits of discipline that were not supported by either devotion or direct personal experience led me to abandon worded prayer altogether for a time.

The reason this gave me pause was that I sensed danger—the danger of assuming that my pattern of growth in prayer should be Su Yin's. My first impulse was to say something that would encourage her movement from what she described as "mechanical" prayer to the new forms of unworded prayer she was beginning to experience. But I hesitated. I needed to be cautious in offering guidance based on my own experience.

Suddenly I was again keenly aware of my inadequacy. Who was I to advise Su Yin as to the best way to deepen her prayer life? I recalled Jesus' warning about the dangers of the blind leading the blind.

But then I became aware of the presence of the Spirit with me as I read the e-mail. The same Spirit who was present with me helping me identify the potential traps in my response was the Spirit who stood ready to offer her the direction Su Yin sought. My role was simply to help her attend to what the Spirit was trying to teach her.

With this freeing realization once again back firmly in consciousness, I replied as follows:

Dear Su Yin:
Rather than offer my own answer to your most important questions, let me suggest that this might be a good time to turn to some guided meditations on the life of Christ. I also think this may be timely as I recall that you wanted to find your way into a deeper love of God, not just knowledge of him. My suggestion is to start a pattern of regular meditation on the Gospel accounts of his life. Select small sections of Scripture, perhaps as short as a verse or even a fragment of a verse. Just allow yourself to enter the scene and observe Jesus. Listen to him. Place yourself in interaction with him and listen to what (if anything) he has to say to you.
Since your immediate question is about prayer, I'd suggest that

you begin with a series of meditations on both the recorded prayers
of Jesus and his teachings on prayer. You can find these easily; so I
will let you select the passages. Rather than analyzing passages,
simply seek to encounter Christ and come to know him better. Let
him set the pace and the direction of this exercise. Simply come to
him asking to learn from him the pattern of prayer that he wills for
you. And let me know the result.
David

Dear David:
Your suggestion has been blessed by God. I began with Jesus' prayer
of John chapter 17. I had been reading recently in John, and this passage has always been a favorite. However, based on your suggestion I
found myself approaching it differently from any previous reading.
My prayer was that I would meet Jesus and learn from him how to
pray. I do not think that this prayer has been totally answered, but I
did feel myself to be listening in on his prayer in a way I have never
experienced before. His prayer for his disciples seemed like a prayer
for me.

   I will continue this exercise. Any observations?
Su Yin

Dear Su Yin:
I fear that any comments I might offer at the moment could get in
the way of the dialogue with Jesus that seems to be developing. I
may have more to say later, but for now just keep following where
the Lord leads and let me know where that takes you.
David

Unlike what I do in counseling or psychotherapy, I do not generally take notes in face-to-face spiritual direction.[1] Nor do I generally reread old messages before responding to new ones when I
work over e-mail. In spite of having a memory that is less than
perfect, even much less than desirable, I count on the Holy Spirit

---

[1]My work with Bill (described in chapters four and five) was an exception to this, as
I informed him that I was writing this book and asked his permission to keep detailed
notes with the possibility of including portions of our work in the book.

to bring to mind what I need to recall from earlier interactions. And he does just that, reminding me of things just when I need to recall them.

During these recent interactions with Su Yin I recalled that she had expressed a desire to deepen her love for the Lord. This was the reason I introduced the idea of meditating on the Gospels. If her love for Jesus were to increase, it would be important for her to spend more time in his presence, meditating on his life and teaching. My suggestion that she begin with his recorded prayers and teaching on prayer was based on her current questions about prayer. But the real point of this exercise is to provide an opportunity for a deeper encounter with Jesus.

Note in these interactions how little work I actually have to do. Clearly Su Yin is moving in her spiritual journey, but the direction for her movement is coming from the Spirit of God. The Spirit has supplied her with her longings, and the Spirit is leading her as she turns to Scripture to encounter Jesus.

The next few e-mails continued our interaction regarding prayer. Su Yin continued to find great profit in meditating on the recorded prayers of Jesus, as well as his teachings on prayer. She also reported a continued deepening of her sense of God's presence with her throughout her day. The tone changed, however, in the next e-mail.

Dear David:
I am sorry I have not written recently, but I have found myself in deep waters spiritually and have not been able to do much of anything. I wouldn't say I am depressed. I recall what that was like when I was a student and have never really encountered that form of despair since then, at least not to the same degree. But I would say that I am spiritually dry. God seems absent; my prayers seem to echo in my head; even Scripture seems irrelevant.

The first thing I noticed as I began to enter this slump was that the daily examen became more and more difficult. I even skipped it on a number of days—this for the first time since I began several months ago. I long for the sense of God's presence that I had. What's going on? Is this demonic opposition? Am I doing something wrong? I know about rhythms of the spiritual life, but this feels darker and deeper than I have experienced since the first year I was a Christian.

Any thoughts or help you can provide?

Su Yin

Dear Su Yin:

When you speak of the rhythms of the spiritual life, you are probably thinking of the fact that spiritual progress seems seldom to be linear, apparent regress often following seeming progress. Forces of spiritual darkness may, in some sense, be ultimately behind this, but I don't think we need to expect to find them directly behind every experience of spiritual dryness or struggle. In my own experience, struggle follows progress as a way of deepening our growth, taking us to a new plateau. I believe that this is what awaits you on the other side of this experience.

How should you relate to this dark night of the soul? As I have already said, I don't personally find it helpful to ferret out demonic forces that may be behind it. You belong to Christ and your life is hid in his Spirit. Trust that he that is in you is greater than he that is in the world. Remind yourself whose you are and trust that nothing can change that fact.

Nor do I find it helpful to attempt to fight the darkness, as if by some effort on your part you can change your present experience. This does not mean that you should not continue to practice the spiritual disciplines you have long practiced and continue to develop but that you should not attempt to do anything to make yourself feel better.

My suggestion is to trust that God is in this experience. Rather than trying to change it, accept it as something he has allowed into your life for your growth. If that is so, it is a gift, and his gifts are always good. Pray for discernment, not to understand what you should be learning from this experience but rather for the ability to see his presence in it and in your life right now.

And know that you are in my prayers.

David

It is always difficult for me to resist efforts to try to help someone struggling. This moment in my work with Su Yin was no different. It is also frightening to suggest that the person try to find God in the midst of the darkness. So often this doesn't seem to work.

But giving advice is not my job in this relationship. My job is spiritual accompaniment with the goal of codiscernment of God's presence. There is nothing more important that I can do than encourage attunement to God's Spirit.

Some people would have answered Su Yin's questions about demonic opposition differently from the way I did. Spiritual direction is inevitably grounded in theology, and my own theological understandings and convictions obviously shape my response. It should never be otherwise. However, my purpose is not to teach theology. It is to accompany Su Yin on the journey that is being led by the Spirit.

Dear David:

Your e-mail was an encouragement to me. It also speaks directly and forcibly to me as what I had been trying to do was change this dark night. My increasing despair was because I did not seem to be able to do anything to change it.

I am somewhat more prepared to live with that if I can really be assured that God is present in it. However, I confess that at this point I can only make that assertion by faith, not by experience. That brings me back to an old question I have been struggling with, doesn't it? I want to know God's presence in the darkness by experience, not simply by affirmation. Is that expecting too much?

Su Yin

Dear Su Yin:

Don't let yourself draw too neat a line between faith and experience. God assures us of his presence in a variety of ways, but we cannot encounter him without faith. So do not try to leave faith behind in an effort to find a basis of faith in some place that is devoid of faith.

But I believe you can know God's presence—and I mean know it, not just believe it to be true. I do not think it is expecting too much

*to ask for that. Pray that you might know that God is with you in
the darkness. Let us ask together that his light may lighten your
darkness just enough for you to catch a glimpse of his presence.*
David

Dear David:

Yesterday was one of the most difficult days I have had in a long
time. All day long I found myself assuring others of things that
seemed far from my personal experience and conviction. I
preached on Romans 8:28-39, a passage I am sure you know well. I
chose this as much for me as for anyone in the congregation. I
needed to be reminded that God is in our darkest moments and
that nothing can remove us from his love. But my words felt hollow.
After lunch I had a counseling appointment with someone in the
congregation who had just received a diagnosis of cancer. She was
filled with despair and anxiety, and although I think I was able to
help her make contact with God in the midst of it, her despair only
seemed to deepen mine. Again I had trouble believing what I found
myself saying to her.

After the evening service I came home and made myself a cup of
tea (something I used to do often in the evening but haven't in the
past few weeks). I then went to the kitchen table and sat down, prepared to spend as long as necessary waiting quietly on God to help
me discern his presence in my day and in my experience of recent
days. My prayer seemed to still be resounding in my head when
suddenly a phrase entered my head—"Darkness is my covering."
My spirit brightened as I said this phrase over several times. I had
no idea where it came from, except I had to trust that the Holy
Spirit had given it to me. It had a biblical ring, but I couldn't recall
where, or if, it was in Scripture. Looking it up in a concordance, I
was thrilled to find it to be a fragment of verse 11 in Psalm 18. "He
made darkness his covering, his canopy around him" [NIV]. I'm not
sure I had ever really noticed this verse, but suddenly it spoke to
me, clearly and powerfully. God is in the darkness! I believe that.
Better, I know that.

Our prayer has begun to be answered. I can't say the darkness is
gone, but—thank God—I can say that I know God is with me in it.

That makes all the difference. Thanks for your prayers.
Su Yin

Dear Su Yin:

*Without trying to second-guess why God has allowed this experi-
ence or what you are supposed to learn from it (speculations that
are, from my point of view, both futile and spiritually distracting),
it may give you an opportunity to learn more of God. Who is this
Christian God who clothes himself in darkness?*

*I wonder if you might find it profitable to take this opportunity to
do some biblical study and reflection on this theme of the hiddenness of God. In working on this, you may also find help from* The
Dark Night *of the Soul by St. John of the Cross. The Cloud of
Unknowing may also be a helpful source. But follow the Spirit in
this and first be sure that he is leading you to pursue such a study.
Let me know what you determine. And don't despair if darkness
returns (as it most certainly will at some point).*
David

This was not the end of Su Yin's dark night of the soul. It lasted
for several more months. But something important had changed.
Most of the time after this point she knew her God was with her.

Following my suggestion that she consider whether this was a
good time for work on the question of the hiddenness or incomprehensibility of God, she began what turned out to be a rich
period of focus on this topic. Over the next several months she
read and reflected a great deal on this, often sharing with me ideas
generated by her work. This led to the following e-mail message
from me.

Dear Su Yin:

*I note in your last several messages a shift from your experience of
God to your ideas about him. I do not mean this as a criticism, and
I think the theological work you are doing is important for you and
has the potential of having significant implications for your ministry. However, I would like to suggest that our conversations might
be even more fruitful if we return to a focus on your experience of*

*God. My question is, how are you currently experiencing God?
What is happening in your prayer life? And what do you think God
is asking of you at present?*

   *Talking about God certainly has a place in our interactions. But I
am even more interested in your evolving relationship with God.
What is happening in that regard now?*
David

Dear David:
Thank you for your gentle reminder not to substitute ideas of God for
experience of him. You know that what I want is to really know him,
not just know about him. And I believe I am making progress in this.

   My study and reading in the last several weeks has reintroduced
mystery into my theology and experience of God. I realize that I had
been cutting God down to a manageable size, ignoring all the parts of
him that didn't fit neatly within my theological boxes. What is happening in my experience of God? I have come to a deeper apprecia-
tion of his majesty. Awe, even fear, is a part of the way in which I
experience God at the present. God is turning up in places where I
never expected him to be. The God who makes darkness his dwelling
is a God who is not easily turned into an idol. This is what I mean by
majesty, awe and even fear.

   So, I continue to come to know him, not just about him. Don't
worry about me getting lost in theology. You know I enjoy it and feel
it to be important. However, I am increasingly discovering what a
poor substitute it is for direct experience of God.
Su Yin

Dear Su Yin:
*I am pleased to hear of where the Spirit has been leading you in
recent days. Your account of what you have come to appreciate
about the majesty of God speaks to me deeply.*

   *What is happening in your prayer life now? And what is your
sense of God's presence throughout the day?*
David

Dear David:
Dare I admit this? I haven't done the daily examen for about a

month now. It just didn't seem helpful or necessary. I guess I already have so many things that I do out of obligation and discipline that I didn't want to add another one to the list. Is this okay or do you want me to resume its practice?

The reason I say that it didn't seem necessary is that I sense God's presence with me much of the time now. This is the most incredible blessing I have received from our work together. I don't mean that I am thinking about God all day long. But somewhere deep within consciousness I am aware that I am in his presence. This seems solid.

As for my prayer life, things seem to be going well. My formal times of prayer begin with gratitude, and this occupies a larger part of these times that has ever been the case before. I find that I have so much to be thankful for, particularly as I thank him for his presence with me in the various situations encountered during the day. (When I say this, I realize that I have incorporated something like the examen into my regular time of prayer.) I continue to pray for a large number of people, but I think I bring less presumption to my prayers of petition. I think my encounter with the majesty of God has made me less demanding of him. I think of it as reminding him of the people he cares for and needs to be sure not to forget. It feels healthier than coming with the feeling that I need to talk him into doing something he probably doesn't want to do. It feels like an important change and I am thankful.
Su Yin

Dear Su Yin:
I think it is quite wonderful the way in which you have incorporated the examen into regular prayer. The important thing is periodic reflection on your experience of God's presence. How you do it is not important.

I also affirm the significance of the shifts that are taking place in your prayer life. Resist the need to analyze it further. Just continue to ask God to teach you how to pray and follow where he leads you.
David

After this last message I didn't hear from Su Yin for six weeks.

This was the longest break in our correspondence to this point. I was just beginning to wonder if I would ever hear from her again when I received the following message.

> Dear David:
> God has been good to me in the weeks since I last wrote. I am learning to trust his presence even when I don't sense it, but much more of the time I find myself aware that he is with me. My heart has been full of gratitude. I find myself offering brief prayers of thanksgiving to God throughout the day. I see God in the lives of the people in our church, and I feel so thankful for the assurance that it is his work in their lives that counts, not mine. And I see God in the world. I look at the people I encounter on the train every day, and I see people with new eyes. I pray that I will see Jesus in those I encounter and often, praise God, I do! It transforms my day. I feel I am surrounded by God's presence wherever I am, whatever I am doing. I am so deeply thankful.
>
> My spiritual life is changing from the discharge of obligations to the offering of joyous service. Even my husband has noticed the difference. He tells me that I am less serious and more relaxed. I think this is true.
>
> I feel so good that I am a bit mistrustful of my feelings. Might I be resting when I should be pressing ahead? Am I avoiding something that I should be facing? I don't want to just coast along. That has never been my style. But I am enjoying God in a way I have never experienced. Any thoughts about what I should be doing next?
> Su Yin

In spite of the fact that I advise others to resist treating questions as things to be answered, I often have to bite my tongue when faced with a series of questions like this. I have opinions on a number of things she questions. And I feel attached to my opinions, easily succumbing to the temptation to view them as reflecting more wisdom than whimsy. But my advice is better than my inclination, even if it is sometimes hard to follow. Su Yin's questions should be prayerfully lived, not simply answered. Any answer must come from the Spirit. I must again bite my tongue.

Dear Su Yin:
I am really pleased to hear that God has given you the gift of grati-
tude. Cherish it and allow it to develop.

However, I am reluctant to attempt to suggest what should be the
next step in your journey. What is the Spirit telling you about this as
you seek God's direction?
David

Dear David:
I understand, of course, that you cannot answer my questions about
what I should next be doing. I have been praying about this question,
and I don't get any answer. I have, however, had a dream that I think
might be revealing. I don't generally recall my dreams, and when I do
they seem to be nothing but nonsense. I also must confess to not
really being comfortable with the emphasis you put on dreams. But
as I say, I did have a dream that was hard to ignore.

For several weeks now I have been asking God to help me know
whether simply to enjoy where I am spiritually or whether I need to
press ahead in some way. This morning I woke up in what seemed to
be the middle of a dream. It was so vivid I had no trouble remembering it. At the center of the dream was a group of children flying kites.
They were in a city square. Strangely, no one else was there except
the children and one old man, watching them from a bench on the
edge of the square. He was smiling and seemed to be enjoying watching the children. One child in particular fascinated me. I have no
idea why. She seemed particularly beautiful and was so happy with
her kite. I felt really drawn to her. I woke up actually feeling a little
sad because she wasn't there. It was quite a dream.

I reread the chapter on dreams in your book and tried to do the
first thing you suggested—the TTAQ technique. The results look like
this:

Title:	Children fly kites
Theme:	Carefree play
Affect:	Joy
Questions:	1. Why was I so attracted to that one little girl?
	2. Do I want to be that little girl?

Is this related to my prayer question?

I am not sure if I am doing this right. But I did want to share this dream with you. Any other thoughts about what questions I should be asking from this dream? I find this the hardest part of the exercise and am not sure I have really understood what you are suggesting.
Su Yin

Dear Su Yin:

Thanks for sharing the dream. What you have done thus far is exactly right. Now you need to ask those questions of God in prayer. Ask him to help you know if this dream was from him and whether it has any relevance to your prayer question.
David

Dear David:

The image of that little girl has stayed with me. I was so attracted to her playfulness—her joy. I have been praying about this, and I believe God is telling me that he is happy to see my joy. Perhaps he is the old man looking on in my dream.

My joy and gratitude continue. However, this does not mean that my life is problem-free. I actually am facing some serious challenges in the church with a fellowship group leader who is causing a lot of trouble. But I am trusting that God is somewhere even in these troubles.
Su Yin

Reflecting on the Portrait

There is nothing mysterious about what I am doing with Su Yin in this series of encounters. I am simply listening to her account of her spiritual experience, helping her focus on that experience and encouraging her to attend to the Spirit of God as he leads her toward himself.

No two spiritual directors will do this in the same way. No one should seek to be like David Benner in how he or she offers spiritual direction. My ways of working reflect my own personality and my own spiritual journey as well as the things I count to be important in

Christ following and spiritual formation. Others will have different emphases and do slightly different things. This is as it should be.

I am quite different with different people. Some people are full of questions and seem to evoke a more directive part of me. Su Yin was such a person. Others share their experience easily and need very little by way of response. I often say even less with these people.

Each person offering spiritual direction needs to find his or her own voice and style. As noted earlier, spiritual direction is not a set of techniques. It is a real person engaging in a real relationship with another person. For each of us, the challenge is the same—to maintain sensitivity to the Spirit and a readiness to follow his lead. We suggest this same thing to those who seek our help. Their task and ours is the same—to attune our souls to God, discern his leading and surrender to his loving will for us.

🏵 How do you understand the dark night of the soul that Su Yin experienced? How have you handled your own dark nights? Think of how others responded to you during these experiences. What things were helpful and what was unhelpful?

7

Becoming a
Spiritual Director

*L*arge numbers of Christians are already engaged in providing informal spiritual guidance to others but have never had a name for it. They may also never have thought of it as a calling. It is just something they do. The discovery of spiritual direction provides a name for their ministry. This is sometimes quite affirming. It also often motivates these people to become better prepared for what they already do.

Others are offering a related form of soul care but, when confronted with the distinctives of spiritual direction, immediately recognize a better fit for their gifts and interests. Often these people tell me that this is exactly what they have long wanted to do but did not know how to prepare for it. Many of these people became counselors because this seemed the best route to what they felt led to do. After some time they began to wonder. The discovery of spiritual direction often produces a clarification of calling.

No one should undertake the work of spiritual direction without the call of God. Recognizing and responding to this call is the first step in preparing for this rewarding and important ministry.

Discerning a Call to Spiritual Direction

How do you know if God is calling you to the work of spiritual direction? I suggest that those called to the work of spiritual direction are generally people who are already doing it in one form or another, who hunger for God and who love people. If these three things are true of you, it may be that this is your calling.

You are already providing spiritual guidance. Calling to the ministry of spiritual direction requires the affirmation of community. Other people help us discern God's gifts and calling. And usually this means that those gifts have already been discerned and you are already providing some form of spiritual guidance.

Sometimes the guidance you provide may occur within your role as a pastor, elder, small group leader or something similar. While you have a great variety of responsibilities, those that involve spending time with individuals for whom you care are especially rewarding. You may describe what you do as "counseling," but there is a good chance that your fulfillment doesn't relate so much to solving problems as to helping people grow. You are good at listening and feel deeply privileged to be able to share people's lives. Although you may have never thought of it as providing spiritual direction, this is exactly what you do. And you do it because people seek you out for it.

Or it may be that you offer your spiritual guidance in informal ways that remain unnamed and generally unnoticed. You may be a pastor's wife or husband whom others seek out for support and guidance. Or perhaps you are a Sunday school teacher or youth worker whose love of those in your charge leads you to extensive involvement in their lives. Or maybe you hold no formal office within your church but others simply seek you out for guidance regarding affairs of the soul.

If any of these things are true of you, others have already noted and affirmed your calling. They observe a degree of spiritual maturity and are able to see something of your commitment to the transformational journey of Christ following. They also see your trustworthiness and interpersonal accessibility. You seem like someone they can feel safe with, and they come to you to share their journey and struggles. They may also affirm your gifts, telling you how comforting they find your presence, how spiritually nurturing they find their conversations with you or how helpful they find your suggestions.

It seems unlikely that someone who has never been affirmed by others in this manner is really called to this ministry of spiritual direction. Such a person may be interested in spiritual direction, but apart from some form of affirmation by their spiritual community, they should not consider it their calling.

You hunger for God. Those called to the ministry of spiritual direction are on a spiritual journey themselves. This means that if this is your calling, you are a person who seeks after God, or perhaps better, hungers for God. If you believe that you have already found him or that your spiritual hunger is satisfied, you have little to offer those who seek to meet God in deeper ways. However, if you long to know God, you may be able to accompany others as they share the quest.

We could describe spiritual directors as persons who, in the language of the New American Standard Bible translation of Acts 17:27, grope after God.[1] One who gropes after God seeks, but as a blind person, without certainty of where God is to be found. Certainty about how and where God is to be found leads to a presumption that interferes with the provision of spiritual direction. God turns up where we least expect to encounter him and often fails to be where we feel most sure he should be.

Groping after God can be thought of as spiritual hunger with humility. If I expect to meet God in exactly the same way and place

---

[1]I thank the Reverend Glenn Mitchell for pointing me to this verse and suggesting its implications for spiritual direction.

where I have met him previously, I make an idol of that experience. I will then usually attempt to get others to worship at my idol and will find it difficult to encourage them to encounter God in other ways and places. If, however, I recognize that the transcendent God who alone fits the shape of the deepest longings of my soul will always be beyond my control, I am no longer surprised when he turns up where I least expect him. I will then be in the best position to accompany others as they seek to meet God more deeply.

Do you continue to hunger and thirst for God? Are you still a seeker, not simply a finder? Do you remain humble about where and how God encounters you? Are you open to the possibility that he will meet others in ways that differ from how he meets you? And do others seek you out for spiritual counsel and support? If so, spiritual direction may well be your calling.

You love people. Finally, those who are called to the work of spiritual direction love other people. Love is the transforming dynamic of Christian spirituality. Christian spiritual formation is training in the school of love. How could we hope to nurture such formation in others if we are not ourselves already making progress in the school of love?

There is no substitute for loving people. If you just love theology, or even if you think you love God but have little genuine love for people, spiritual direction is not your calling. Nor is it your calling if you simply love seeing people grow, giving them help or solving problems. What you must love are ordinary people just as they are. How tragic it is that some people have spiritual influence over others and yet lack love for them. Any significant encounter with such a person damages one's personhood.

This does not mean that you will immediately love every person you encounter. I encounter some people who are difficult to love, and I am sure others feel the same about me from time to time. The love that we offer others is God's love for them. We must desire that love to be ours if we are to help people encounter and surrender to divine love.

If, in addition to the things we have already considered, you love people and find them interesting, your calling may include the ministry of spiritual direction. You will recognize this by noting that you enjoy sharing people's journeys and entering into their experiences. You count doing so to be a privilege, not merely a responsibility or an obligation. And you do so because you genuinely love people—not just people in general but the people whose lives touch yours in particular.

An Illustration

Juliet, my wife, has been providing spiritual nurture and guidance to others for all of her adult life. Only in the last several years has she begun to connect it to spiritual direction, and only within that time has she come to understand that it forms an integral part of her calling.

Juliet has always loved people. Her care for her friends and family has been consistent and creative. Small acts of thoughtfulness for others fill her day. Hers is not the self-serving love of the emotionally needy person who needs love in return. Of course, being human, she loves to be loved. But she does not need a return on the love she invests in others. Love is, for Juliet, its own reward.

Juliet's love of God has long been the passion underlying her love of others. It is also the passion that fuels her spiritual journey. Her spiritual pilgrimage is a journey of a lover with, and at the same time toward, her Loved One. Her love of God is clear to others, not simply from her words but by her quiet, attuned spirit.

Talking with Juliet has always been easy. Perhaps the greatest gift she gives others in conversation is her presence. She is deeply present and deeply interested. Her inner stillness offers others a momentary quiet. Being with her is restorative.

For these and many other reasons, people have always sought out Juliet for friendship and conversation. At times they sought her counsel, but often just her presence and friendship. Often these were friendships characterized by mutuality. Other times they were relationships of nurture and support.

Juliet's interest in spiritual direction arose within the context of the contemplative retreats she and I have led. As part of these, retreatants often seek us out for prayer and conversation. Juliet wished to prepare herself better for this work. She also longed for a deepening of her own intimacy with God. She and I had practiced a form of mutual spousal spiritual direction that I will describe in chapter nine. But now she felt that it was important to find another spiritual director, someone other than her husband.

She began her search for a spiritual director by visiting a nearby Catholic retreat center, where she met a nun who said she was willing to work with her. They agreed to an initial meeting to explore this possibility. Following this and a period of prayerful reflection, Juliet agreed to a series of four sessions one month apart. At the end of these she and her spiritual director agreed to embark on a more intensive experience—one year of weekly sessions (and daily times of meditation and journaling) built on the Ignatian spiritual exercises.[2]

Juliet's experience over the course of that year was profound. Listen in on a segment of my conversation with her about it.

David: How has your experience in spiritual direction affected you?

Juliet: It has done more to change me and my experience of God than anything else in my life. Most important is that I have come to know both myself and God much more deeply. Painful as it has been, God has helped me see through many of my most important self-deceptions. A lot of what I have been learning is about discernment—seeing Satan's deceptions as well as those of my own making for what they are and learning to discern and surrender to the leading of the Spirit.

---

[2]Although these exercises have historically been conducted in the context of a thirty-day retreat, St. Ignatius anticipated current time pressures enough to suggest a framework for this less intensive but more extended adaptation of the classic approach. Each approach has both advantages and disadvantages.

David: How does that relate to discerning a call to the work of spiritual direction?

Juliet: Clarification of my calling was never the primary goal of my spiritual direction. My goal was a deeper knowledge of God. But because God can't be known apart from surrender to his will, discernment of his will and clarification of my calling were always part of our focus. The big question was my willingness to choose his will over mine—to surrender to his desires for me. As I was able to choose more and more of that surrender, I feel he has shown me more and more of my calling. Increasingly, I understand that to include being a spiritual companion for people. I am still unclear about how I am to fulfill this calling and whether to pursue further training. So stay tuned and we will see where God leads!

The majority of the spiritual companionship Juliet currently offers is not packaged as "spiritual direction." Most people who meet regularly with her for prayer and conversation simply think of her as their friend. As she says, what it is called is much less important that what it is. But what she is called to do is important, and she now knows that serving as a sacred companion forms an important part of her calling.

Preparation for Providing Spiritual Direction

Perhaps you, like Juliet, are already providing spiritual companionship for people, love people and have a deep longing to know God. Perhaps you wonder whether spiritual direction is more central to your calling than you had realized. What next steps should you take? As was the case for Juliet, preparation usually starts with a personal experience of spiritual direction.

Personal experience in spiritual direction. Finding a spiritual director can sometimes be challenging. My first experience in direction was in the middle of the 1980s, when there were fewer trained directors and fewer resources for identifying them. I had been reading books on the topic and longed for a deeper experience of God. I approached my pastor—the Reverend Robert Harvey, to whom this book is dedicated—and asked if he would serve as my spiritual director. He and I had often discussed books on the topic, as we were both interested in learning more about it.

He agreed to serve as my spiritual director on one condition—that I would agree to subsequently serve as his. We met with each other weekly for the next year. For the first six months he served as my spiritual director; for the second I served as his. At the beginning neither of us knew anything about spiritual direction beyond what we had read. By the end of the year, however, both of us had learned a great deal about ourselves, God and the process of giving and receiving spiritual accompaniment.

Although working with a better-trained director might have been preferable, the Spirit made powerful use of this experience of weekly prayer and conversation with a godly man. First and foremost, I found my way into a deeper encounter with God. That, after all, was the reason I had sought out spiritual direction. However, I also learned a good deal about how to use spiritual direction. I came to learn how to be more honest with myself and God about the affairs of my soul. I also learned how to attend to the presence and leading of the Spirit, how to use Scripture for personal spiritual direction and a great deal about how to pray.

I also began to get some ideas about how to accompany someone else on a spiritual journey. My friend brought gentleness and presence that I deeply admired but often lacked. My temptation was to trust my understanding. Watching him taught me to trust the Spirit. I also learned an enormous amount by observing the way he related to Scripture as a source of guidance. Never using it as either a club or a support of personal authority, he repeatedly led us both back to Scripture when we sought answers to important questions. He truly was not the director. Rather, he was a guide, leading us both to a focused attention on the Spirit and the Word.

In reality, as long as there are trustworthy, mature Christians, there are potential spiritual directors. Increasingly, however, it is possible to find people with formal training. Numerous spiritual-direction training programs exist across North America, and denominational and other directories identify graduates who are qualified and willing to provide spiritual direction. While the process of identifying the right director may take some time, no one needs to assume that there are no qualified spiritual directors available. Internet listings even identify people willing to provide spiritual direction by e-mail or phone.

In seeking out a potential spiritual director, don't assume that he or she needs to be in your denomination or share all aspects of your theology. Remember that spiritual direction is not primarily about theology. It is about personal, experiential encounter with God. No one should allow petty denominational differences to stand in the way of the growth and learning that can come through a relationship of spiritual companionship with a wise, mature Christian, even if he or she swims in a different part of the Christian pond from yours. Actually it is often preferable that the spiritual director not experience God in precisely the same way as you.

Understanding the dynamics of the soul. The second way to prepare to provide spiritual direction is to increase your understanding of what I call the dynamics of the soul. Spiritual direction involves the deepest parts of human personhood. The more you know about the psychospiritual functioning of persons, the better a guide you will be in the affairs of the soul.

I use the word *psychospiritual* to emphasize the fact that the soul does not have separate compartments for psychological and spiritual aspects of functioning. This means that the understanding of the soul that is necessary for those who provide spiritual direction is both psychologically and spiritually informed.

Christians seeking to equip themselves for work in soul care often approach the study of psychology primarily out of interest in its therapeutic technologies. They want to learn such things as how to counsel, when to refer or how to diagnose. While there is enormous value in such technical skills, people easily overlook the more basic importance of gaining an understanding of the psychological dynamics of the inner world.

Over the course of the last hundred years psychology has added immeasurably to our understanding of obsessions, guilt, anxiety, forgiveness, envy, addictions, fear, jealousy, compulsions, worry, shame, depression and a host of other matters. Similarly, an understanding of the mental mechanisms of defense (including denial, rationalization, repression, suppression, reaction formation, splitting and the like) helps one understand how the inner world operates not simply psychologically but also spiritually. Those who provide spiritual direction routinely encounter such dynamics, and their ability to help is enormously facilitated by understanding.

But psychological understanding that ignores spiritual dynamics is in itself incomplete. Knowledge of the spiritual dynamics of the soul is also essential. This is best gained by either formal or informal study in Christian spiritual theology and formation. Such study helps one understand such things as doubt, the development of faith, prayer, blocks to experiencing God, varieties of spiritual experience, sin, spiritual longings, mystical experience and a range of related phenomena. Those who provide spiritual direction are aided in both their own spiritual journey and their capacity to help others on that journey by their understanding of the dynamics of spiritual formation.

Psychology and theology both provide road maps of the soul. Who would think of attempting to lead someone else through a country that they did not know thoroughly? Spiritual directors need the help of the best maps of the soul that are available. None are comprehensive. All are incomplete. Some may even be, in certain respects, misleading. But studied carefully, all contribute to our understanding of the dynamics of the soul. No spiritual director can afford to be ignorant of them.

An immense literature exists on the psychological and spiritual dynamics of the soul. A smaller body of literature seeks to begin to integrate the psychological and spiritual aspects of functioning. No comprehensive integration has yet been accomplished. Help in getting started in the study of the dynamics of the soul is provided in the "Suggestions for Further Reading" section at the end of the book.

Commitment to a deepening knowledge of self and God. I have earlier referred to the importance of knowing both God and self and have written on this more extensively in my book *Care of Souls.* Why is this is so important?

Those who seek to guide others in the affairs of the soul must be in a place of ever-deepening knowledge of both themselves and God. A shallow knowledge of yourself limits you to a shallow knowledge of God. Similarly, a shallow knowledge of God limits you to a shallow knowledge of self. As noted by John Calvin, deep knowledge of either requires deep knowledge of the other.

Too often Christians who know a good deal about God are held back from a more intimate knowing of him by a corresponding lack of intimate knowing of themselves. They run from any frank encounter with their depths. Inner places of darkness and pain frighten them, and they avoid their inner world. Their understanding of their particular patterns of sin is limited, as is their awareness of the nature and meaning of their deepest longings. They know little about their characteristic patterns of self-deception and think of honesty primarily in terms of not telling lies to others. In short, they know little of their own soul.

Others have spent too long looking at themselves and not enough looking at God. They may have information about God but have little personal knowledge of him. They may have a regular pattern of prayer but spend this time talking, never having learned to listen. Their intimate knowing of God is limited, and this will limit their knowing of themselves.

Those who seek to care for the souls of others must learn to take care of their own souls. The single most important way they do this is by a commitment to an ever-deepening knowing of themselves and God. This is a lifelong commitment. A person does not simply take a course or a degree and get this done. Spiritual directors are not necessarily farther along in this journey than those they seek to help. It is often helpful if they are, but I am convinced it is not necessary. What is necessary is that they be committed to the lifelong process of knowing self and God.

Knowledge of Scripture and grounding in theology. Having emphasized the value of the study of psychology and spirituality, I should also make clear the importance of the study of Scripture. The point of such study for the spiritual director is not primarily learning theology but coming to know God. This reminds us that the God we must come to know is uniquely revealed in his Word. Even though the Word became flesh, we must start our knowing of the Word in Scripture, not simply in our inner experience.

However, this does not mean that theology is unimportant to the work of spiritual direction. If held with humility, theology provides the spiritual director with a framework for organizing personal experience of God. Spiritual directors do not need to be experts in theology. Nor, in my opinion, is formal theological training a necessity. However, they should be sufficiently well grounded in theology to have a framework for understanding the work of spiritual transformation as well as its obstacles.

Skill in holy listening. One of the core skills of the spiritual director is what Margaret Guenther calls holy listening.[3] She describes holy listening as presence and attentiveness. The goal of holy listening is not hearing information but facilitating contact between the person and God. It could therefore also be described as facilitative listening—listening that facilitates awareness of the presence of God.

Most people think they already are good listeners. They may

---

[3]Margaret Guenther, *Holy Listening: The Art of Spiritual Direction* (Boston: Cowley, 1992).

have learned to be reasonably attentive when others speak and assume that this is all that is involved. However, what they are often listening to is their own thoughts about what they are hearing. This is different from the listening that spiritual directors need to offer.

Others have had training in empathic listening, perhaps as part of counselor preparation or in some other communication training experience. They have learned to not only be attentive but to tune in to unexpressed feelings. They have also learned to communicate back what they are hearing in ways that foster exploration. There is much value in such listening. But the listening required in spiritual direction involves more than empathy. In fact, empathy for the one you are seeking to help can be a distraction.

As noted earlier, the real focus of the director's attention should be the Spirit of God and the other person's experience of God. Their emotions may form a part of this experience, but their emotions are not in themselves the primary focus of spiritual direction. Training in empathic or therapeutic listening can be of great value for spiritual directors if they understand the differences between counseling and spiritual guidance. In fact, it is often the most readily available means of gaining training in listening.

Even apart from formal training, however, it is possible to gain skills in the holy listening that is involved in spiritual direction. The best place to practice it is in other soul friendships. Try speaking less and listening more. Practice being fully present to the other person, setting aside your private preoccupations and feelings, and making yourself available for the Spirit. And most important, begin learning to listen to the Spirit and the other person at the same time. Be attentive to God's presence yourself, and seek to be attentive to the presence of God with and in the one to whom you listen. This is holy listening. By means of it you help the other person increase awareness of God's presence, and this, as I have noted, is central to spiritual transformation.

Training and supervision. Although some people—myself included—provide spiritual direction without the benefit of formal training, it is encouraging to see increasing numbers of people choosing to undertake structured preparation. Options for doing so range from weekend seminars to graduate degrees. Numerous non-degree certification programs also exist, often two-year programs that include personal spiritual direction, coursework and supervised experience in providing spiritual direction for others. Information about these is easily accessed via the Internet.

Another way training can sometimes be arranged is through a person who provides spiritual direction and is willing to offer an individualized apprenticeship. If you have not had a previous experience of personal spiritual direction, this may well be the best first step. Once this is completed, a period of supervision of your own work in spiritual direction can then sometimes be arranged.

The role of retreats in preparation for spiritual direction should also be noted. The most famous and best developed of these is the classic thirty-day Ignatian retreat. Built on the spiritual exercises of St. Ignatius, this retreat provides an opportunity for intensive spiritual direction. Many formal training programs in spiritual direction require the thirty-day retreat. As noted earlier, this retreat can also usually be completed on a less intensive basis over a longer period of time.

Those serious about their preparation for the important work of spiritual direction should earnestly consider formal training. At this point the field is unregulated, and anyone can call himself or herself a spiritual director. However, the responsibility of spiritual companionship is a serious one, and the best preparation possible is usually the best advice.

Preparation for the work of spiritual direction is lifelong. Even a Ph.D. in spiritual formation does not complete the preparation that is needed. Soul work with others who seek to know God more deeply and surrender more fully to his love demands that you remain on an ongoing journey of preparation—not simply for spiritual direction but for personal wholeness and holiness.

Reflecting on the Call to Spiritual Direction

Those called to the practice of spiritual direction are usually already providing it in some form. Others have recognized their love of God and people and seek them out for conversation, encouragement and spiritual counsel. Sometimes this is in formal and structured relationships of spiritual accompaniment, while at other times it is in informal relationships of friendship. But regardless of what it has been called, they have been providing sacred companionship to others.

❋ If this is true of you, how does the spiritual accompaniment you provide fit with your sense of calling? Prayerfully reflect on any stirrings you detect in your soul after reading this chapter. What next steps do you feel led to take? Share these with someone whose spiritual companionship you trust.

Becoming a spiritual director usually begins with a personal experience in spiritual direction. There is no better way one's call to this form of soul care can be confirmed than in such a relationship. But more important, there is no better way you can gain a deeper knowledge of both God and self than with the accompaniment of a sacred companion.

❋ If you find yourself drawn to the idea of receiving spiritual direction, prayerfully reflect on whether this might be the leading of the Spirit. Talk with someone who either has received or offers spiritual direction to further explore this possibility.

❋ Reflect on your own knowing of God and self. Where are you most deficient? What steps could you take to begin to remedy this?

Sharing the spiritual journey with another person is a high privilege. Not everyone is called to the formal work of spiritual direction. But all of us are called to a spiritual journey that cannot be undertaken without companionship.

Spiritual accompaniment takes many forms. Some of them combine spiritual friendship and direction. Small groups and marriage offer unique possibilities for such a combination, and we turn to these applications in the next two chapters.

Part Three

COMBINING
SPIRITUAL FRIENDSHIP
& DIRECTION

8

Spiritual Accompaniment in Small Groups

While it excites me to see increasing numbers of people pursuing training in individualized spiritual direction, this is not my great hope for the church. There are simply too many Christians who could benefit from spiritual direction to expect that they will all find individual directors.

A significant part of my hope for the church lies in the small group movement that has already had a significant impact around the world. Millions of Christians meet regularly with a group of other Christians, and for many of them this is already the most important support they have for their spiritual journey. Having been a member of a small group fellowship for most of the past three decades, I count myself among them. Talking and praying together, supporting each other through life crises, studying Scripture or other Christian literature, many of us have already discovered the great value of spiritual companionship.

But because small groups typically serve a variety of purposes, they often have awakened rather than satisfied people's hunger for an intimate soul friendship. They have also probably done a better job of fostering fellowship than of providing genuine spiritual direction.

Yet the potential of small groups as a vehicle for spiritual accompaniment is enormous. In fact, small groups are probably the most readily available means of providing spiritual friendship and direction. To fill this role, however, they must be structured and run in a manner that best suits this purpose.

Spiritual Accompaniment Groups

Small groups exist for a variety of reasons. In some churches they serve administrative and pastoral-care functions, keeping track of members and ensuring their spiritual support and nurture. Often their primary purpose is the support of Christian discipleship and spiritual formation. Some are primarily designed for fellowship. Still others have prayer as their main purpose.

This chapter focuses on groups designed to combine spiritual friendship and direction. Although these groups involve a form of fellowship, what they strive to facilitate is soul friendships rather than spiritual acquaintances. Bible study typically does not play a major role in such groups, as they are less oriented toward content than toward experience. Prayer is, however, central to them. And if they are designed and run with care, experience in prayer can be the means by which group members increase their attunement to God, attention to his Spirit and willingness to surrender to his will.

There is no single way to run spiritual accompaniment groups. I will not therefore present a detailed plan for how they should be structured. Groups designed for this purpose do, however, share at least four common features.

The priority of questions over answers. The wise person recognizes that questions are often more important than answers. When someone asks, "What is the meaning of life?" he or she should not be given an answer but encouraged to explore the question. To offer an answer is to shut down the quest and stifle the spiritual hunger that it reflects.

Some Christians are overly concerned about answering questions. They treat questions as the enemy—something to be eliminated. They are uncomfortable leaving answers unstated or ambiguous. They worry that an unanswered question may lead someone to a wrong answer. Such people must have a great deal of difficulty with Christ's typical methods of discourse. Frequently he answered questions with a question. Even more often he answered with a parable—a paradoxical story that yields its meaning only on careful reflection.

Jesus knew the value of a good question. In fact, on several occasions he turned someone else's statement into a question, introducing uncertainty where previously there had been only certainty. Think, for example, of the person who came to Jesus to report that his mother and brothers were outside looking for him (Mark 3:31-34). In response Christ asked, "Who are my mother and my brothers?" Then to ensure that the question accomplished its purpose, he followed it with the paradoxical gesture of pointing to those surrounding him and asserting that these were his mother and brothers.

The spiritual journey inevitably confronts all of us with questions that need to be expressed and lived, not simply answered. No one should try to answer questions such as "Where was God when my child died?" "Why is this happening to me?" or "What should I learn from this experience?" What is needed is a patient, listening presence that remains open to the person and encourages him or her to remain open to the questions and to God.

People whose questions are answered rather than honored often stop asking questions—at least of those who give answers. They may worry that their questions are being interpreted as signs of doubt or a lack of maturity. Or they may simply stop asking questions because they are tired of the answers. Others take their questions elsewhere, often moving outside the faith community to find others who are less invested in a destination and more committed to the journey, to any journey. All these outcomes are tragic.

The church should be the place where questions are welcomed. And a small group designed to support the spiritual journey will take care to honor questions and be careful never to try to simply answer them.

While writing these last few paragraphs, I have been thinking of several Christian friends. Three years ago Tony left his evangelical church for a mainline congregation because he needed a place where his questions would be accepted, not answered. His faith was in a process of transition. It was not in any serious trouble. He remains a keen Christian. But he needed people around him who would take his questions seriously enough to explore them with him. What he wanted was dialogue. Tragically, he did not find it in his old church or in the groups he had been a part of in that congregation.

I also think of Anna, who has an active mind and a questing spirituality. Her participation in a spiritual accompaniment group keeps her in her church and the faith. Her experience of her church as a whole generally provides more irritation than spiritual nurture. But she remains because several people express care for her by their commitment to journey with her as spiritual friends.

The church should be a home for spiritual seekers, not simply spiritual finders. It should be a place that encourages the spiritual quest. Small groups that offer spiritual accompaniment should, in particular, welcome those who are spiritually longing and restless. If satisfaction has replaced longing and certainty has eliminated questions, a spiritual way station has supplanted a spiritual journey.

Prayerful listening. When small groups are designed primarily for spiritual formation purposes, content often becomes more important than process. The goal becomes acquiring understanding of biblical truths or mastery of spiritual disciplines. These are important and valuable ends. But they are not the ones that are most appropriate for a spiritual accompaniment group. A group designed for spiritual accompaniment has as its goal the development of a climate of prayerful listening to each other and God.

As noted earlier, *prayerful* refers to the fact that those who seek to offer spiritual accompaniment are themselves attentive to God. Spiritual accompaniment occurs within a context of prayer. When I open myself to my friend—seeing him through God's eyes or hearing her through God's ears—I am in prayer. Julian of Norwich describes the process of prayerful attentiveness to another as involving a continuous looking back and forth between God and the other person. Prayerful attentiveness is prayer.

Prayerful attentiveness is cultivated within a climate that honors silence. It is often helpful to begin spiritual accompaniment groups with silent prayer. Each person is encouraged to become still before God and aware of his presence. In silence each person seeks to attend to God's Spirit—in him or herself, in the others in the group and in their experience together.

Because prayerful attentiveness begins with attentiveness to God, I like to begin group sessions with a *lectio divina*. Literally meaning "divine reading," this ancient Christian practice involves a prayerful listening to Scripture, or as it is usually described, praying Scripture. Lectio divina is grounded in a balance of silence and the Word. Listening always involves silence. The listening to Scripture that is at the core of the lectio divina is a listening in silence and stillness that seeks to encounter God as he speaks directly and personally to you.

Lectio divina involves listening to the reading of a short passage or a few isolated verses of Scripture. Those who listen are encouraged to set aside analysis, and even understanding, seeking instead to open themselves to God's Word and receive it expectantly and passively. They then attend to what they receive from God. God's Word is received personally, as an individualized gift to each person.

After hearing the passage read, the classic form of the lectio[1] involves asking participants to sit in silence before God, noticing whatever captures their attention in the passage or in their inner experience. The passage is then reread and the process repeated.

---

[1]Norvene Vest, *Gathered in the Word: Praying the Scripture in Small Groups* (Nashville: Upper Room, 1996).

This time, after a silence, participants are asked if they wish to share a single word or phrase that particularly strikes them as they listen. No further discussion occurs. After another moment of silent prayer the passage is then read again. This time people are given an opportunity to speak briefly of how the passage seems to touch their lives. Finally, after a fourth reading they are asked to share what they feel the passage might be inviting them to do.

Corinne Ware[2] describes a modification of the classic lectio that many people find helpful. It emphasizes four ways of reading (or listening to) Scripture, each named for the corresponding monastic form of meditation. It also involves reading the passage four times. The instructions I use for each reading in this method are as follows.

1. *Lectio.* Listen with your senses, without thinking too much about the meaning. Attend to your imagination, noting the smells, sounds and images that arise as you hear the passage. Allow yourself to enter into the setting using your imagination.

2. *Meditatio.* This time I want you to follow along in your Bible as I read the passage out loud. Use your thinking to reflect on the meaning and significance of the passage. Consider why the passage is included in Scripture. What does it mean? How does it affect your understanding of God?

3. *Oratio.* This time as you listen, I want you to attend to your feelings. Note your feelings and silently offer them back to God as a prayer of the heart. Comment in your prayer on anything in the passage to which you particularly respond.

4. *Contemplatio.* Before I read the passage a final time, quieten yourself, close your eyes, breathe deeply and regularly, and prepare to receive God's Word. This time I want you to listen with your intuition—your heart. If something impresses you, simply notice it and then refocus your attention on what you are hearing. Don't worry if you do not seem to have any thoughts or impressions. Sim-

---

[2]Corinne Ware, *Discover Your Spiritual Type: A Guide to Individual and Congregational Growth* (Bethesda, Md.: Alban Institute, 1995.)

ply remain open to the passage and to the Spirit. After expressing gratitude to God for your experience, open your eyes.

Beginning a group with a lectio divina orients participants to God and his Word and establishes a culture that honors silence and attentiveness. This is the foundation of prayerful listening. Listening is at the heart of spiritual accompaniment groups. This is what gives such groups their contemplative character. This is also why silence is so important. Describing such listening as "prayerful listening" reminds us that while group members listen to each other, they also listen to God. The two are deeply compatible. As I listen to you in prayer, I remain attentive to God—particularly to his presence in you and in whatever you are sharing.

Sharing spiritual experience. Spiritual accompaniment groups give priority to the use of group time for speaking of spiritual experience. This does not mean that someone can never tell of a job loss, exciting family news or other important recent experiences. But when such external events are shared, the focus should be the participant's experience of God in the midst of these life circumstances. This marks the most important difference between a spiritual accompaniment group and one that is organized for general fellowship.

Group members often find it helpful to prepare for group meetings by reflecting and journaling on where God is in their experience. Questions such as the following can assist this preparation:

- What do I think God has been trying to say to me in the recent past?
- How has God been present for me in recent weeks?
- When did God seem to be absent?
- What spiritual practices have been particularly meaningful to me in recent weeks?
- Which have been less meaningful than usual?
- What do I seek from God at this point in my life?

Group members who reflect on questions such as these before the meeting come prepared to share their experience of God, not simply their life experience. And they come better able to attend to God's presence in the experience of those with whom they journey.

After beginning with the lectio divina exercise, I generally invite people to speak briefly of what has been occurring in their faith journey since we last met. I encourage people to listen to each other in silence rather than interrupting with questions or comments.[3] When the first person has completed what he or she has to say, I invite all participants again to enter a minute of silent prayer, seeking to heighten their attentiveness to God. Group members then can engage in dialogue with the first person. Again, this dialogue should be focused on the experience of God, not the life circumstances that form the context. After a suitable period I again invite people to enter a moment of silence, followed by an invitation for someone else to share.

This is far from the only way to run a group that seeks to support spiritual accompaniment. Most such groups are probably run with less structure and less use of silence than what I have just described. I have participated in such groups and have no quarrel with conducting them in such a way. But the contemplative style of group that is built around silence is particularly useful in heightening prayerful attentiveness to God and each other. It is therefore a style that I find especially suitable for groups that are designed to combine spiritual friendship and direction.

The climate of support and acceptance. Richard Foster makes a suggestion for spiritual formation groups that I think is at least as relevant for spiritual accompaniment groups: "Give encouragement as often as possible; advice, once in a while; reproof, only when absolutely necessary, and judgment, never."[4] This would be an excellent motto for all spiritual accompaniment groups.

Spiritual accompaniment is accompaniment in love. Love is the

---

[3]This pattern of listening and silence draws on suggestions made by Rose Mary Dougherty, *Group Spiritual Direction* (New York: Paulist, 1995).

[4]Richard Foster, foreword to *A Spiritual Formation Workbook* by James Bryan Smith and Lynda Graybeal (San Francisco: HarperSanFrancisco, 1999), p. 9.

motive for attentive listening. Love is the motive for offering atten-tiveness to the Spirit instead of mere advice. Love is the motive for any reproof that must be given. And love is the motive for the over-all climate of encouragement and support.

What I want from a spiritual accompaniment group is support and acceptance. I do not primarily look to my group for advice, although I am open to that if it is given sparingly and if I ask for it. But generally that is not what I want. As I think is true for most people, I generally know what to do. Doing it is the challenge.

Although I do not come to the group wanting reproof, I really do want my friends to help me keep on the path and not get lost in my self-deceptions. Love means that if I need to be challenged about something, I am much more likely to receive it well. I may not ini-tially welcome it, but I am almost certain to hear it eventually if it is offered in love. And I, like you, am pretty good at telling when that is true.

Spiritual accompaniment occurs when people who love and are committed to each other pledge themselves to the support of each other's spiritual journey. This is the primary purpose and dynamic of a spiritual accompaniment group.

Starting a Spiritual Accompaniment Group

The spiritual intimacy that forms the core of a spiritual accompani-ment group demands a high degree of trust and compatibility. The starting point in establishing a group is identifying at least one other person with whom you feel trust and a desire to share your own spiritual experience. You may or may not know that person well at this point. However, you probably feel attracted to him or her and sense the possibility of being a kindred spirit. Pray about the choice of this person before approaching him or her, and then arrange a time to get together and discuss your vision.

If the other person is not familiar with this book, it might be helpful to suggest that he or she read it before you meet. You will then have at least some common ground in your expectations and understanding of what such a group involves. Don't let yourself become preoccupied with questions of mechanics or structure in this first discussion. Keep the focus on vision. Tell the other person what you seek in terms of spiritual accompaniment, and see if he or she shares some of the same deep desires.

Avoid pressing for a commitment. Remember, you have likely been thinking about this idea longer than the person you have just approached. If, however, he or she is interested, agree to pray about it for a while and then get together and discuss it further. This interval may be a good time for you both to do some thinking about size, structure and other potential members.

If, as sometimes happens, the other person immediately responds with interest, you already have a group. You may chose to make it bigger, or you may chose to simply start with a group of two. Keep in mind, however, Jesus' promise that where two or three people are gathered in his name he is in their midst. A group of two becomes therefore a group of three: Jesus walks with you as you seek to discern his presence and respond to his call.

Ideal size and membership. If spiritual accompaniment groups can be as small as two, what is their ideal size? The optimal size is probably between three and five members. The maximum is probably six. When groups are larger than this, it becomes difficult for everyone to share. It also becomes easier to hide.

Ideals of membership are harder to describe. In my experience there is no need to restrict membership to a single gender. Although initial intimacy often develops more quickly when the group is composed of only men or only women, the richness of the accompaniment is sometimes more limited in such groups. Ultimately, however, other criteria for who should be invited are more important than gender.

Another common question is whether husbands and wives should be in the same group. My advice is to not mix couples and noncouples. Couples already share a good deal of intimacy, and their presence tends to unbalance a group that has a mix of couples and noncouples. However, some people will want their spouse to be involved. If this is the case, the possibility of a group composed of two or three couples should be considered.

Couples bring a complication to spiritual accompaniment groups. Seldom are spouses at the same point in the spiritual journey, and often they have differing interests in spiritual accompaniment. Couples groups thus have some disadvantages over groups that do not include couples. Paradoxically, they sometimes have trouble developing the deeper levels of intimacy that groups without couples can experience. However, they also have several advantages. The biggest of these is that, sharing the experience of the group, each couple has an opportunity to deepen their own spousal soul friendship.

The most important membership criteria relate to compatibility, the presence of a desire for spiritual accompaniment and the willingness to support prayerfully others on their journey. Age, gender, marital status, socioeconomic status and even level of spiritual maturity all are of minor importance compared to these matters. The group is not a microcosm of the church, and diversity is not therefore as important as it is at the level of the congregation. Compatibility is more important. The vulnerability that must necessarily mark a spiritual accompaniment group demands that people feel safe with each other. For this reason it is often easier to start with two people and add members one at a time, as led by prayer and careful reflection on the question of compatibility.

Compatibility does not mean homogeneity. In fact it would not be a good idea to attempt to form a group of people who are like each other in spiritual style or personality. That would rob the group of the benefits of differing perspectives. However, it is crucial that people feel comfortable with each other. Sharing the intimacies of one's spiritual journey puts a much higher demand on relationships than sharing study of the Bible. Do not make the mistake of assuming that any group of five or six people should be able to share their inner worlds in the way I have described in this book.

Prayerful support of the spiritual journey of the other group members is built on a commitment to pray for each other between sessions. Apart from this, the accompaniment is limited. However, when people are committed to supporting each other in regular prayer, the accompaniment is not limited to the relatively few hours they are actually together.

Form and structure. The optimal schedule is probably something like two meetings a month, each lasting approximately two hours. Shorter sessions do not allow everyone time to share, and longer or more frequent sessions are seldom feasible given other time commitments. Whereas Bible studies and other spiritual formation groups often meet weekly, this is generally too often for the sort of sharing that should be a part of a spiritual accompaniment group. People need time to have spiritual experience between group sessions if they are to have something to share when they meet. Some groups even find monthly meetings to be ideal.

The bulk of the time in any meeting of a spiritual accompaniment group should be used in sharing and listening. Each person should be given an opportunity to share in each meeting, although there should be no pressure to do so. Sharing should be understood as an opportunity for a spiritual update, not a report of recent spiritual triumphs. For the group to be successful, members must be able to feel safe enough to report honestly whatever is actually going on in their lives. Pretense does not foster growth.

I recommend ending group sessions with ten to fifteen minutes of prayer. Ideally this should take the form of members' praying for each other, focusing on things that have been shared.

One final matter of form that is worth noting is the value of a ritual such as lighting a candle when the group is ready to begin. A simple act such as this clearly marks the end of informal visiting and boisterous conversation, serving as an invitation to still ourselves before God and prepare to hear his Word. Some groups also value saying the Lord's Prayer as a closing.

These practices may seem inconsequential and even mechanical. They serve, however, to set apart the time as something special—different from a normal evening of conversation.

Leadership. Leadership of a spiritual accompaniment group is important. Leaderless groups do not work as well as those with a designated leader. The responsibility can be rotated, but a designated leader for each session is important.

The leader's responsibilities include

◉ opening the session

◉ selecting the Scripture passage and leading the lectio divina

◉ maintaining an appropriate balance of talking, listening and silent prayer

◉ maintaining the flow of sharing

◉ closing the session

◉ ensuring that the time and location for the next session are identified before the group disbands

The leader should not be expected to serve as the spiritual director for the group. Nor should the leader be expected to have to sacrifice group involvement. The responsibilities are administrative and not incompatible with regular participation. The only exception to this is that sometimes it is difficult to both conduct the lectio divina and fully experience the spiritual benefits of the exercise.

What to Expect from a Spiritual Accompaniment Group

When coming to a new group, most people tend to bring hopes shaped by the best of past group experiences and fears associated with the worst. In the face of this, many approach a new group with cautious expectations. But what can a member reasonably expect from a spiritual accompaniment group?

First, a spiritual accompaniment group is an excellent place to expect to find spiritual friendship. It is a place where people express their commitment to each other through prayerful interest and support in each other's spiritual journey. I may not become best friends with any of the people in my group. Nor may I experience as much intimacy as I might like. But I can reasonably expect to find people who will share my spiritual journey and allow me to share theirs. This is the core of soul friendship.

Second, it is reasonable to expect that the group will change over time. Don't join a spiritual accompaniment group if you want it and the pattern of relationships within it to remain static. The nature of the spiritual journey is that people will change. Some may change in ways that lead them away from the group. Others may journey to places quite different from where your journey takes you. Don't allow yourself to become sentimentally attached to how the group was at some point in the past. A spiritual accompaniment group is, like life itself, dynamic and ever-changing.

Third, you should expect it to be a place that will help you attune to God's Spirit as you seek to discern his call and surrender to his love. Some groups specialize in helping people develop spiritual disciplines, others in engaging with God's Word, and yet others in nurturing an experience of fellowship. Spiritual accompaniment groups specialize in helping people attune their spirits to God's Spirit. Put another way, what you should expect is growth in discernment— discernment of God's presence, call and will.

No one should expect a spiritual accompaniment group to replace the church. Nor will it necessarily eliminate the value of membership in other kinds of small Christian groups. Each kind of group meets certain needs of certain people at certain points in their lives. Spiritual accompaniment groups are not in any way superior to other groups. They are just different. And in being so, they offer something that other types of groups do not generally offer as well.

Group Spiritual Accompaniment Illustrated

The meeting we will look in on occurred after a group had been together for several years. It was originally made up of people who had participated in various retreats and workshops that I had offered. I served as the initial leader, but after a while the leadership rotated among the other group members. The group consisted of six members—Mike, Elena, Wes, Sara, Anna and I. Meetings were held once a month for an hour and a half.

In the previous session Mike had told us of a lurking sense of mistrust that had crept into his relationship with God. God had not seemed to hear his prayers regarding a problem he had been experiencing, and this was beginning to affect his trust in God. Mike also spoke of feeling uncomfortable at the thought that God was always watching him, a point that had been raised in a recent sermon.

Elena (serving as the leader this meeting) began the session with a lectio divina based on Psalm 139:1-6 (NIV).

> O LORD, you have searched me
> > and you know me.
> You know when I sit and when I rise;
> > you perceive my thoughts from afar.
> You discern my going out and my lying down;
> > you are familiar with all my ways.
> Before a word is on my tongue
> > you know it completely, O LORD.
>
> You hem me in—behind and before;
> > you have laid your hand upon me.
> Such knowledge is too wonderful for me,
> > too lofty for me to attain.

After a silence and a second reading she asked people if they wished to share a word or phrase that was particularly striking to them.

Mike: Too wonderful!
Wes: Pass.
Sara: You have laid your hand on me.
Anna: Lying down.
David: You hem me in.
Elena: Your hand is on me.

After another period of silence Elena read the passage a third

time. She then asked if anyone wished to share what he or she
heard.

Mike: Well, the first time I heard the passage I didn't hear anything addressed specifically to me. As I told you, what
struck me were the words "too wonderful"! I also felt
myself smiling. The third time I felt a really warm sense of
God's love. It's quite wonderful! It gave me a sense of comfort knowing that God is watching me.

Sara: That's really great. I have been praying for you about that.

Mike: Thanks. It really means a lot to me that you heard what I
said and remembered to pray.

Elena: Who else received something from God that they would
like to share?

Wes: I can't say I heard anything in tonight's passage. I heard
the words, but there was nothing that stood out for me
tonight.

Elena: Okay, anybody else?

David: The first time you read the passage, the phrase that spoke
to me was "you hem me in." The second time the same
words struck me, and I felt myself relax. That feeling deepened with the third reading. I'm left with a wonderful
sense of God's love. Strange, but it feels great to be
hemmed in.

Elena: That was the phrase that I heard the first time as I read the
passage. But the second time it was "your hand is on me."
That really speaks to me. It assures me that God's presence
isn't just something mental, it's real—it's physical.

    Elena suggested a couple of moments of silent prayer. She then
read the passage a fourth and final time. After a moment she asked
if anyone felt God offering them an invitation of any sort in his
Word to them.

Wes: Well, that was pretty weird! The last time you read it, I
had a sense of God's hand on my shoulder. [Laughing] I'm
not going crazy, am I, Doc? But it did seem that God was

present, not in words but in some more physical way.

Elena: Was there an invitation in that?

Wes: I don't know. Perhaps "Trust me."

Elena: Okay. Anybody else?

Sara: I envy Wes. I heard the words but didn't get the kinesthetic version of the message. But I too had a sense of comfort from God's presence. I still hear God saying, "I have my hand on you." It's really comforting.

Anna: The invitation I received in that passage was to let go. Like Wes, what I received was also more of a sense than a word. I heard "lie down" each time the passage was read, but what I felt was a letting go. The invitation was to let go.

David: Any idea about what you are being asked to let go of?

Anna: Maybe effort, maybe thinking, maybe so much doing. I don't know. But I don't want to think too much about it. I just want to do it. Maybe then I'll understand it.

This sharing continued for a few more moments before Elena suggested another moment of silent prayer. Afterward she asked who would like to share about his or her spiritual experience in recent weeks.

Sara: Well, I'll start. Last night I reviewed my journal entries for the last month. It was an interesting exercise. The big thing I have been dealing with since we last met was confusion about my job. You all know about that, and nothing is new. I'm still afraid to quit before I find something else, but I hate my work more and more. But that isn't what I have been journaling about. In my journal I have been talking with God about the whole situation—about how I should pray, about how to know his will, about what I want to do with the rest of my life—all sorts of things related to the job and situation. What I noticed when I reread the recent entries last night was that my prayers had slowly begun to shift from "What should I do?" to "How can I know you and your will more clearly?" I still need and want help around the job. But I think I also am beginning to want to know God and his will for me even more than wanting out of the job. Don't get me wrong. This isn't the whole story, but I do detect something beginning to shift.

Elena asked the rest of us to spend a moment or two in silent prayer, focusing our attention on God and his presence in Sara's experience. After several minutes she invited response to Sara. No one immediately said anything, and she began herself.

Elena: I'm not sure how you recognize this new level of desire to know God, particularly when you continue to feel the same need for an answer to the question about the job. What exactly has changed? Can you say more about that?

Sara: I'm not sure if I can describe it, but let me try. I still pray for God's help in knowing what to do. But I have been getting frustrated with that prayer because he doesn't seem to answer it. I guess that led to my journaling about what I should be praying for. And the more I thought about that, the more I began to recognize that I was simply using God as a job-finding resource. What I seemed to want was another job, not to know God and his will for me. This was a bit of a shock. I confessed this to God, and slowly I began to notice a change. Increasingly I found myself praying that I would know him better. I still pray for help in knowing what to do with the job, but right at the moment knowing him has become almost as important. [Laughs] I know it should be *more* important, but I'm trying to be honest. But it is a change, and it seems to me to be important.

Elena: I think it is important. I do the same thing. I pray for blessings much more than I pray for a deeper encounter with God. I don't think I really believe that getting God himself would be as good a deal as getting the things I need from him. Pretty shocking realization, isn't it?

David: I think we all face the same doubt. You have expressed it really well, but it is true for me as well.

Anna: I like how you put that, Elena. I think that hits the nail on
the head for me. I generally think that I know best what
God should give me. Most of the time I want his gifts more
than I want him. I find that a really depressing thought.

Conversation continued along this line for another five or ten
minutes. Elena then exercised her responsibility as timekeeper for
the evening and suggested a moment of silent prayer before asking
who else wanted to share recent spiritual experience.

Reflecting on Group Accompaniment

There are no spiritual giants in this group. It is a group of ordinary
Christians, serious about growing spiritually and committed to
doing it together. We have learned that in daring to meet each other
in honesty and vulnerability, we also meet God. And we have
learned that as our friendship with each other deepens, so too does
our friendship with the Lord.

❖ Evaluate Christian small group experiences you have had in the
light of the four ideals of spiritual accompaniment groups. Which
would you personally find the hardest to implement? Which would
you personally find most helpful?

❖ What possibilities do you see in lectio divina as part of a spiritual
accompaniment group? If you have never experienced this, consider putting together a small group that would meet for three or
four occasions simply to experiment with this means of encountering God's Word.

Spiritual accompaniment can be as simple as two people agree-
ing to meet regularly and share their spiritual experience. These
times can be structured in a great variety of ways. There is no single
correct way. The focus, however, needs to be God. And the role that
each person plays needs to be that of a humble pilgrim who both
offers and receives support for the spiritual journey. This is the core
of being a sacred companion.

9

Spiritual
Accompaniment
in Marriage

I recently gave a lecture on spouses as soul friends and was surprised by a strong objection to the idea from a Christian psychologist in the audience. She argued that couples already have enough pressure on them to make their marriage work without adding the romantic expectations of being soul friends. She urged me to be realistic and scrap such lofty ideals.

Not surprisingly, further discussion with this woman revealed that her own marriage was seriously lacking in intimacy. Furthermore, she had long abandoned expectations of its ever returning. What she envisaged as the ideal marriage was a pragmatic partnership—a functional relationship that would optimally support parenting and household management. I found that a chilling vision.

This sort of resignation to reduced expectations is tragically common. It should not, however, obscure the enormous potential of spiritual friendship in marriage. Make no mistake about it: spousal spiritual friendship represents a high ideal. In marriage, with the multiple levels of intimacy that can and should exist, spiritual friendship cannot exist apart from more general soul friendship. However, ideals should not be abandoned just because they are difficult, or even sometimes impossible, to achieve.

Supporting the Development of a Spousal Soul Friendship

Achieve, however, is not quite the right word to describe the development of a soul friendship. Such a relationship is always a gift to be received, not simply an end to be accomplished. The most we can do is encourage its development and then thank God if he graces us with the blessing of such a friendship.

However, better than marrying with the hope that my spouse will become my soul friend is first to nurture the development of a genuine friendship and then marry as a way of deepening it. Romance does not automatically translate into friendship. Friendship requires cultivation. Couples who seek to develop genuine intimacy in a range of spheres of life—not simply to be dragged toward marriage by the heat of their passions—are well on the way to receiving the gift of a soul friend, not simply a romantic partner or spouse.

Attraction and compatibility are an insufficient foundation for marriage. The first fruits of a real friendship are a much better predictor of the future of a marriage than the passion of a hot love.

Marriage will never automatically produce soul friendship. Nor is it helpful to demand that my spouse be my soul friend. Even a sense of entitlement to a spousal soul friendship can work against its occurring. Quite simply, there is nothing I can do to manufacture a soul friendship. But I can nurture the soil out of which such a relationship may develop. I do this by cultivating three things—respect, an absence of control and dialogue.

Respect. Respecting my spouse sounds simple, yet it is extremely demanding. Sometimes we confuse respect with the feeling of love. Genuine love includes respect, but it is alarming how many people feel some form of love for their spouse and yet offer rather low levels of respect.

Respect for my spouse begins with respect for her separateness from me. Love based on enmeshment—a kind of blurring of the boundaries between my spouse and me—is not love but narcissistic self-gratification. As already noted, if I am to love another person, I must first respect the fact that he or she is separate from me.

Even the term *my husband* or *my wife* carries potentially dangerous connotations of possession. Our husbands and wives are not our possessions. Nor are they extensions of us. My wife is separate from me. And until that fact is firmly secure in my consciousness, I can never proceed to enjoy the fruits of a genuine friendship.

An awareness of separateness is perhaps even more important in spousal soul friendship than among those who are not married. The intimacy of marriage makes it easier for couples to see their spouse as an extension of themselves. The one-flesh biblical metaphor for marriage does not mean a fusion of two people that results in a loss of the identity of either or both. The image of becoming one flesh affirms the depth of the shared intimacy that God intends. However, it should never be understood to suggest that two people become one person. Healthy soul friendships include space in the intimacy. The foundation of a genuine spiritual friendship is a togetherness that respects separateness.

Closely related to this, another dimension of the respect that is essential for the development of a soul friendship is respect for my spouse's uniqueness. *Unique* means more than *separate*. It also means *different*. Respect for this uniqueness is not a grudging acknowledgment of something I have come to realize I cannot change. It means honoring and affirming this uniqueness. It means abandoning efforts to make her like me. At core it means prizing her uniqueness by nurturing and supporting it.

It amazes me how often men are blissfully unaware of their wife's uniqueness. They fail to notice the pattern of personal preferences, attitudes and values that lie behind accommodations to their own. They also fail to recognize that these differences reflect the contours of a person who is quite distinct. The exception to this is, of course,

when such a man is fighting with his wife. At this point he is preoccupied with the differences, blaming his wife for being different and
making this the scapegoat for all their problems. Wives, of course,
can be guilty of the same thing. The challenge facing both men and
women is the same—to pay loving attention to the ways in which
our spouse differs from us and then to honor these differences.

The Christian foundation for respecting a spouse's uniqueness
and separateness is seeing him or her through God's eyes. Chapter
two noted the importance in dialogue of seeing another person
through God's eyes. The reason is that such a vision serves as a
foundation for respect. As soon as I see my spouse through God's
eyes, I see her as a unique creation of God, called from eternity to
be the special and distinctive expression of the face of God that she
is. Obviously she is therefore separate from me. And obviously, her
separateness and distinctiveness are things that I should prize. If
God values these distinctives, how can I do less? This is the basis of
my respect for her uniqueness.

When I see my wife through God's eyes, I see her in God and God
in her. This helps me step back a bit and introduces the space we
need in our togetherness. It also protects me from seeing her as an
extension of myself. Even more, it protects me from seeing her as a
possession. She is God's special creation, temporarily loaned to me
for the special one-flesh intimacy of a marital soul friendship.

Seeing a spouse through God's eyes also involves sensitivity to
his or her spiritual journey. Being attentive to this journey is foundational to spiritual friendship, as this is what allows spouses to
journey together. Journeying together as soul friends does not mean
simply sharing parenting or other domestic responsibilities. It
means supporting each other's spiritual journey. And attentiveness
to this comes from seeing your spouse as God sees him or her.

You may ask how you can see your spouse as God does. This perspective comes only from prayer. Concern for my wife's spiritual
journey leads me to pray regularly for her, asking that I will be able
to discern the Spirit's presence and activity in her life and thereby

support, never obstruct, the Spirit. The more I pray for her, the more I see her as God sees her—through eyes of love and concern for her spiritual growth. I also begin to be able to discern God's vision for her. Spiritual friendship is aligning myself with this vision—taking care to facilitate it however I can.

This gift of discernment forms an important part of all genuinely spiritual friendships. Spiritual friends are attentive to the activity of the Spirit in each other's life. By means of this attentiveness, they also help each other be more discerning of the presence and leading of the Spirit. This attentiveness to the presence of the Spirit forms the basis of the Christian's respect for the separateness and uniqueness of his or her spouse.

Seeing God in your spouse is a transforming vision. One of the truly astounding passages in the New Testament is Christ's assertion that whenever we encounter another person in need, we encounter Christ, and what we offer in response to that need we offer to Christ. In Matthew 25:31-46 Jesus teaches that his primary postresurrection presence in the world today is in the person who is needy. Seeing my wife through God's eyes is a powerful way of seeing not just her value but also her needs. In such a view I see her vulnerability, her brokenness and her neediness. This is Christ in her.

Contrary to expectations, the Lord of the universe appears to us not primarily in experiences of success and power but in brokenness and need. To see my spouse as God sees her is therefore to see Christ in her. It provides the basis of the respect I attempt to show her as my spiritual friend.

Absence of control. A second element that is foundational to the development of a marital soul friendship is an absence of control. This begins with the abandonment of all agendas for change of the other person. We are often tempted to think that love gives us the right to work toward what we perceive to be improvement in our spouse. But this is manipulation. It has no place in a genuine soul friendship.

Spiritual friends love each other as they are. Seeing each other through God's eyes means they increasingly see glimmers of what God is doing in the spouse as he calls him or her to wholeness and holiness. My role is neither to suggest the agendas for change nor to ensure that change happens. Those responsibilities belong to the Holy Spirit.

An absence of control also means an absence of possessiveness. If my spouse is not an object that I possess but a person with whom I share a journey, what healthy place can there be for feelings of possessiveness? Such feelings always reflect a need for personal soul work, as they reveal the presence of a destructive agenda of control.

A much more obvious sign of desire to control is any form of coercion or manipulation. It amazes me that God, who has all power at his command, refuses to use that power to make me do the things he wants me to do. God's restraint is an excellent model for soul friends. But many of us often unconsciously go through our days moving people around like objects and using whatever power or influence we have to get people to do whatever we think they should do. It is not surprising, then, that this spills over into marriage.

Even in good marriages spouses often behave in ways intended to pressure each other. This is manipulation. Whether it takes the form of emotional manipulation or physical coercion, it is always destructive. Genuine spiritual friendships wither under conditions of coercion and manipulation. They flourish under conditions of the abandonment of such control.

Dialogue. Dialogue is the most important thing that soul friends actually do with each other. But all couples talk with and, at least to some extent, listen to each other. How does the dialogue that supports the growth of spiritual friendship differ from the conversations that other couples have?

Dialogue begins with active listening. It demands attentiveness and engagement that are unlike what we typically offer each other under the guise of listening. We are all far too good at listening with one ear while continuing to remain busily engaged with other things. We easily slip into the bad habit of "listening" to each other while continuing to read the paper or work on the computer or remaining engaged with other mental or physical chores.

Couples on their way to the establishment of a soul friendship are committed to the discipline of really listening to each other. They know the importance of taking time to sit down and face each other during important conversations. They have begun to make progress in setting aside inner mental distractions and genuinely making themselves available to their spouse. And they have learned that this is hard work that will require ongoing commitment and discipline.

The second characteristic of dialogue that supports the growth of soul friendships is that it is deeply valued by the couple. While many couples make an effort to maintain communication because they know it is important, those on their way to becoming soul friends talk with and listen to each other simply because they enjoy the other person's presence. The attractiveness of their spouse is such that they want to know him or her better. They also want to share things about themselves and to explore things with their mate.

Desire, curiosity and passion drive dialogue. It is the route to new places, new understandings and new vistas on self and the world. No one needs to tell such a couple that dialogue is a good thing. They long to spend time conversing with each other because of the intrinsic rewards associated with doing so. This does not mean that these people spend all their time talking with each other or even all their time with each other. Marriage requires rhythms of talking and quietness, togetherness and separateness. Spouses cultivating spiritual friendship value all these things.

Spouses making progress toward spiritual friendship take risks in their dialogue. They share their real feelings and opinions. They do not hedge their bets. Because they trust their spouse and are learning to feel increasingly safe in being vulnerable with him or her, they share parts of themselves that they would otherwise hide. Feelings of shame or guilt that would naturally make them want to run and hide are sometimes shared in an act of enormous trust. The discovery that the sharing of such feelings is rewarded with deepened self-understanding and intimacy leads soul friends to take the risk of sharing more and more of themselves.

This does not mean that everything is shared. Recall the place of separateness in even the most intimate human relationships. Attempts to share absolutely everything are naive and quickly over-load the circuits. But soul friends dare to let each other into the parts of themselves that normally are so private that we choose to ignore them.

One of the risks associated with dialogue is the risk of change. Genuine dialogue requires that I be willing to change my point of view. If I am not open to such a possibility, the most I can engage in is conversation about my point of view or debate or discussion as a means to attempt to convince the other of it. Dialogue demands that both parties be willing to see themselves and the world differently because of the engagement.

Every time I engage in genuine dialogue with my wife, something in me changes. She and her experience become a part of me. This may result in a change in my opinions or feelings. But more profoundly, it may result in a change in how I see the world, her, the issues we are exploring and even myself. Such growth and change are part of the journey.

Fear of the risk of change keeps some people in a safe place at one of the many convenient way stations on the journey. But it means they are unable to experience the intimacy and rewards of spiritual friendship with their spouse.

The Ecstasy of Spiritual Union
I have already noted how spheres of intimacy naturally seek to expand and, when they do, serve to reinforce each other. Christian singles who seek to live within the ethical framework of the Bible

will limit their sexual intimacy, as its fullest expression is restricted to marriage. Spousal soul intimacy requires no such restriction and allows for the fullest possible emergence of intimacy across all spheres of human experience.

The Song of Songs (or, as it is known in some translations, the Song of Solomon) is a tribute to the exquisite charms of erotic love, particularly as experienced within marriage. Its passages are filled with rich allusions to longing, passion and ecstasy. It reads as one of the great love poems of all time. And it is in the Bible!

Sexuality is God's gift, just like dialogue and friendship. And when they come together in marriage, the result is an intimacy of unequaled proportions. In the words of the Song of Songs, it is "more delightful than wine" (1:2) and "strong as Death" (8:6); "the flash of it is a flash of fire" (8:6). Indeed "love no flood can quench, no torrents drown. Were a man to offer all the wealth of his house to buy love, contempt is all he would purchase" (8:7). Of such incalculable worth is love!

Sexuality is intended to form an important part of spousal soul friendship. The Song of Songs should not be treated as merely an allegorical reference to the relationship of the church and Christ. It is a poetic tribute to erotic love within spiritual union of two people in marital soul friendship.

But marital sexuality can never hope to reach the lofty summits of ecstasy and passion described in the Song of Songs unless it is united with respect and dialogue. Genuine sexual intimacy cannot occur apart from intimacy in a variety of other spheres of life. Sexual intercourse then holds the possibility of being not simply the joining of two bodies but the joining of two souls. Apart from this, sexuality regresses into sensuality. Only when it is situated within the rich tapestry of other forms of nonerotic engagement does it have a chance to reach its full potential.

Sexual passion is a woefully inadequate foundation for a spousal soul friendship. It is, however, a singularly rich and life-enhancing capstone.

Spousal Spiritual Friendship

I began this chapter by suggesting that marriage offers unique opportunities for spiritual friendship. Susan and Paul's story nicely illustrates this possibility.

Susan and Paul are easily recognized as having a soul friendship, not merely a successful marriage. Those who know them even casually can't help but notice their comfort with each other, the absence of any hostility in their interaction, the depth of their respect and love for each other, and how much they enjoy being together. One of the reasons these things are obvious with them is that Paul and Susan have been married to each other for nearly forty years. The long years of nurturing the development of a soul friendship have had ample time to bear fruit, and the fruit that has been born is ripe, mature and obviously quite special.

Early patterns. Currently aged sixty-two and sixty-four respectively, Paul and Susan were married in their early twenties just after he completed a degree in engineering. Susan was already teaching, and they began their marriage with both working long hours to get established in their jobs. Friends who knew them at this point of their marriage describe them as obviously in love but not noticeably different from any other young couple. This matches Paul and Susan's recollection of this stage of their marriage. Looking back, they believe they were both probably more focused on their jobs than they should have been, but they did love each other deeply and set out to build a marriage that would last.

One of the things they did to attempt to achieve this became a pattern of their relationship that continues today. From the first year of marriage Susan and Paul resolved to set aside weekly quality time to continue to get to know each other. In the early years this took the form of one quiet evening a week when they unplugged the phone, lingered over dinner and spent several hours getting caught up on what was going on in each other's life.

When the first of their three children arrived, this became more difficult. However, apart from occasional weeks where days and nights of hectic demands flowed into each other without interruption, most weeks of most months of most years included the one sacred evening when they shared at least an hour of good dialogue. As the children grew a little older and Susan and Paul's income made it possible for the couple to eat out more, the pattern became a once-a-week dinner in some quiet, favorite restaurant. This continues to the present. The core element of the evening, however, is not the dinner but the opportunity it provides for extended, relaxed soul conversation.

My guess is that this, more than anything else, is the reason Paul and Susan are so comfortable with each other. Merely surviving forty years of marriage is not enough to guarantee the development of a spiritual friendship. Less time is, on the other hand, more than adequate if that time has been invested in the nurture of soul intimacy that is based on respect and an absence of manipulation or control.

I mentioned that Susan and Paul enjoy each other's company. The reason this is so obvious to others is that they share their company with others much of the time. They have always deeply valued their friends and spent a lot of time with them. Their love for each other has never been something exclusive that makes them withdraw from others. Rather, it seems to energize them for engagement with others.

But in contrast to some couples who spend time with others as a way of avoiding being alone together, Susan and Paul love to spend time together. For years they have chosen to drive whenever they travel within the country. This gives them long uninterrupted days together on the road, something they both deeply value. These road trips have become their customary form of vacation—the trip being the holiday, not merely the mode of transportation.

Road trips are adventures, and any couple who has made them knows of the potential frustrations that abound in such adventures. To love taking such trips together has always seemed to me to be a wonderful sign of their friendship.

Another noteworthy quality of their friendship is their shared sense of humor. Both have a sparkle in their eyes that reflects an ever-ready ability to take themselves and their experiences lightly. This allows them to see humor in situations that would otherwise look serious. Both laugh easily with others, and when they are together, their humor is infectious. In contrast to private humor that separates, their humor spills out in ways that pull others in rather than pushing them away.

Real people/real struggles. Paul and Susan do not have a perfect marriage, nor is their friendship something out of a romance novel. They are real people, and their relationship has experienced challenges. The absence of a need to idealize each other, themselves or the relationship allows them to talk openly about these challenges with those they know and trust. To their circle of friends they have no need to appear perfect.

Paul is able to describe candidly the effort it took not to withdraw from his wife after he experienced the devastation of a late-career dismissal from his job. During this time he struggled with depression and found himself, for the first time in his life, pulling back from those he loved and who loved him. This was new and confusing for both him and Susan. But their commitment to continue to talk with each other about whatever was going on in their lives ensured that ultimately this struggle only strengthened their marriage.

Susan's biggest struggle occurred a few years ago when a tumor was found in one of her breasts. Since she was apparently coping well with the treatment, tests and uncertainty, her friends were surprised when she told us how irrationally angry with Paul she was feeling. But again, her commitment to the marriage and to honesty and openness with her soul friend meant that ultimately this too only served to strengthen their relationship.

In many ways Paul and Susan appear as one person. They fit so well together that it is hard to think of them as being separate. But the greatest likelihood is that one of them will die before the other, and they will then be separated. How will they cope, particularly since they have been so close and their lives so intertwined?

I think they will cope well. Although they experience the intimacy of the biblical one-flesh ideal, they are in fact separate people. They have learned to honor this, not just tolerate it. There is no possessiveness in their relationship. Nor is there any control. Instead each affirms the other's personal journey and is clear about the fact that it is not his or her own.

For a male of his generation and cultural background, Paul has done particularly well with this. He has always encouraged Susan to have her own friends, to remain active in organizations associated with her own interests and to go away on spiritual retreats as a way of attending to her spiritual journey.

Although Susan encouraged the same things, Paul needed more prodding to follow this advice. By nature he is content and somewhat passive. Consequently Susan has always had to encourage him to maintain a life of his own, separate from their shared life. In recent years he has been doing better at this. He now attends a men's group at church that he had previously neglected in favor of couples activities. After a medical checkup identified elevated cholesterol and blood-pressure levels, he also joined a fitness club and has begun to develop new male friendships there.

The friendship that Paul and Susan have is special but not unique. Nor is this kind of friendship limited to those who have been married for many years. But their friendship reminds me that soul friendships are not automatically a part of marriage, even a good marriage.

Too many people have stable but unsatisfactory marriages. They settle for too little. Dreams of being soul friends to each other seem too idealistic, so they content themselves with the more limited demands of maintaining appearances and a reasonable quality of intimacy. Marital soul friendships are challenging, but they are possible. As Susan and Paul illustrate, they do not require perfection— just commitment and hard work.

Marriage is in many ways the ideal context for soul friendships. Tragically, this is seldom realized. Couples settle for marriages that survive or merely minimize conflict and maximize happiness. Spousal soul friends refuse to settle for this. They have the opportunity to experience the ecstasy of a spiritual union that combines dialogue and intimacy in a broad range of spheres of life. These are the ingredients of a marital soul union. Its joys and blessings are among God's best gifts.

Spousal Spiritual Direction

I haven't described the details of the spiritual sharing that exists between Susan and Paul because I don't know them. There is, however, one marriage where I do know those details well enough to have something to share. Written with the collaboration of my wife, here is the story of our own efforts to combine spiritual friendship and direction.

Most people who know that Juliet and I have been attempting to offer each other spiritual direction have responded with some mixture of amazement, concern and interest. A common reaction has been that the idea sounds intriguing but it definitely would not work for their own marriage. Some have expressed concern about what they perceive to be a blurring of boundaries and potential overloading of emotional circuits. Many have expressed deep interest in what we are attempting.

Until recently we have generally been reluctant to share much of this with others. In spite of leading public lives, we are both uncomfortable drawing attention to ourselves. Far from setting ourselves up as having an ideal marriage, we are painfully aware of our failings in soul accompaniment and intimacy.

But we do enjoy the blessing of a soul friendship. Juliet is, and has been for many years, my closest friend. And I am deeply privileged to be the same for her. This led to our initial efforts to offer each other spiritual direction. On the urging of some people who have learned of these efforts and the hope that broader sharing may encourage others to attempt their own experiments, I offer the following to illustrate the possibilities of spousal spiritual direction.

Building a Soul Friendship

Neither of us would characterize the early years of our marriage as involving a genuine soul friendship. We were deeply in love, and they were wonderful years of our journey together. But while we were laying the foundations for a solid marriage, it would be misleading to suggest that we were actually experiencing soul intimacy. Swept along through the early stages of the family developmental cycle, we were caught up in our young love and the pressures of early careers. We were developing patterns of deepening intimacy in a range of spheres of life, but we certainly did not achieve this instantly.

The journey toward spiritual intimacy was uneven. Having devotions together—either as a couple or later as a family—never worked for us in the early years. Numerous efforts only led increasing to frustration. Finally, we abandoned the effort. This was probably a good thing, at least for that stage of our life together.

We never, however, abandoned dialogue. And our dialogue always included rich and extended discussions of our inner world and experience, spiritual experience always being central to this. We worked hard to cultivate emotional intimacy, as we recognized that apart from this our spiritual intimacy would always be limited. Intellectual intimacy came easily, as we were always voracious readers and we discussed most of the things we read. We also cultivated the habit of regular consumption—and discussion—of movies. Decades of this experience have provided wonderfully fertile soil for spiritual dialogue.

I acknowledge with embarrassment, however, that we recovered shared worded prayer as a regular discipline only as we approached the empty-nest stage of family life. Having only one child got us to this point faster than otherwise would have been the case. But it was still longer than would have been ideal. By this point we were beginning to colead retreats for others, and leading guided retreats for each other was our first experience in mutual spiritual direction.

Guided retreats. Juliet recognized the value of regular personal retreats before I did. She asked me to help her structure the first one. She was planning a one-week experience of solitude in a setting several hours from our home. She asked me to help her identify some readings and areas for prayerful reflection that might focus the spiritual work she hoped to do during her days away.

We discussed and prayed about this for quite a while before this first retreat. I encouraged her to attend to the leading of the Spirit in her life. I also asked her to identify what she felt she most wanted from God. Out of this she gradually identified a book she wanted to make a central part of her focus for the week (Thomas Merton's *New Seeds of Contemplation*), a theme she wished to pursue in Bible study and prayerful reflection (knowing God with the senses, not just the mind) and a structure (daily hikes and times of reading, prayer and journaling). We agreed that I would join her on the last day for a time of extended processing of her experience.

This first foray into spiritual direction went very well, given how little we knew about what we were doing. What we got right in that first experience was to trust the direction of the Spirit. The Spirit, always dependable in the role of spiritual director, led Juliet to and through a precious experience of God in those five days. And the privilege of sharing in this with her did much to deepen our spiritual friendship.

Soon it was my turn. I began to plan a three-day solo sailing trip on Lake Ontario. But unlike other singled-handed sails that I had undertaken for adventure, this one was to be structured around purposes of a spiritual retreat. Now it was Juliet's turn to help me prepare. And when I returned, it was her turn to help me debrief as I shared my experience of God in those days of first retreat.

The pattern was now firmly in place. In one way or another Juliet would undertake periodic retreats on land, and I began what has become a ten-year tradition of sailing retreats on the water—anchored in a lagoon of an island at night and alone with my God on the waters during the day. And we continued offering each other spiritual direction around these experiences.

Habits of the soul. During this time we continued to share the affairs of our inner world on an ongoing basis. For years we have both had the habit of ending our day sitting in bed, each writing in a journal. As we do this, we often share insights, discoveries and spiritual struggles. Our dialogue with God in our journals often is extended to dialogue with each other. Never simply handing over our journals and always respecting the sacred privacy that they represent, we do frequently share portions of what we have written in them.

For years we have also both practiced the daily examen (examination of consciousness) as part of our nighttime ritual. Reflecting on our experience of God's presence with us during the day, we often share this. Occasionally we pray together to end the day, but this still remains sporadic. We are not spiritual giants. We are simply trying to cultivate habits that nurture our spiritual friendship as well as our own and each other's soul.

Structured appointments. The most recent development has been the establishment of regular sessions in which Juliet provides me with spiritual direction. She already had another spiritual director so did not need me for this ongoing role. She does, however, regularly tell me about her experience in spiritual direction, and we pray together about things she is working on as part of this.

I had not had a formal relationship of regular spiritual direction for a number of years. I asked her therefore if we could meet once a month for spiritual direction. After exploring with me what I wanted from God and hoped for from the experience and from her, she agreed. We have now been doing this now for nearly two years—with some frustration but also to great profit on my part.

The major frustration has been on my part also. I am often unsure what to share over dinner and what to save for our monthly structured appointments. Some things demand sharing immediately—both blessings and struggles. Other things are better saved for the leisure of the hour that Juliet devotes to prayerful attentiveness to my experience of God's Spirit. Knowing which things are which has not always been clear. At times separating them out has been a bit artificial. But the frustration has been small compared to the blessings.

Juliet begins and ends each of our spiritual direction sessions with prayer for me. She then invites me to tell her something of my recent experience of God. I generally do so by consulting my journal and reading portions of recent entries. In these monthly meetings—as opposed to daily conversations—I have the opportunity to reflect on the big picture of my recent spiritual experience. These are rich opportunities to reflect prayerfully on what I believe God has been teaching me and how I have been responding. They also provide a wonderful opportunity to reflect on patterns of my spiritual life.

Sometimes these conversations are as short as twenty minutes. Seldom are they longer than an hour. Sometimes I am bursting with things to share. Other times I keep the appointment more as a discipline that is good for my soul than as a time keenly anticipated. Never, however, do I experience less than a warm and welcome encounter with God and a reminder of my wife's concern for my spiritual well-being.

To this point we have resisted the temptation to make these times more mutual. I do not pray for her in them. She prays for me. These times are for me. She is there for me and me alone. If and when she wants me to provide regular spiritual direction for her, we will do that at a separate time. While mutual spiritual direction seems possible, neither of us sees how it could fail to be seriously diluted if we were to combine direction for each other within a single occasion.

What we are doing is not unique and certainly not an illustration of some ideal pattern. Undoubtedly many couples are doing a better job of offering each other spiritual accompaniment. I know of one couple who have a "date" every night to share their experience of God during the day. Others must be doing the same in one way or another. Our structure is working well for us at the present, but we may not continue it indefinitely. Sharing our experience, I hope, will encourage others to share theirs.

Different stages of marriage offer different challenges and opportunities for spiritual friendship and direction. The early years of marriage are the perfect time to establish a genuine friendship. If spiritual intimacy is interwoven in the fabric of other forms of intimacy, a husband and wife are well on their way to developing a relationship that should be capable of sustaining their shared journey over a lifetime. Formal efforts to provide each other with spiritual direction are, however, probably premature in the early years.

Later stages of marriage offer their own challenges but generally provide more potential for spiritual direction. Each couple will have to work out the pattern of how to do this for themselves. What my wife and I have been attempting probably requires an egalitarian marriage. Other models of marriage would likely require some modification of what we have been doing. But spiritual intimacy can occur within any marriage if both partners desire it and are willing to take the risks that it involves.

Reflecting on Marital Accompaniment

Marriage offers rich and unique opportunities for both spiritual friendship and direction. The base on which these possibilities must always be established is a foundation of spousal soul friendship.

If you are married, reflect on the quality of the friendship that you and your spouse share. How has that friendship changed over the years of your relationship? What would you have to do to deepen it? Reflect and journal on these questions, and then seek an opportunity to discuss them with your spouse.

For couples with a reasonable base of security and maturity, the opportunity to develop a more formal relationship of spiritual direction holds exciting possibilities.

▣ What possibilities, if any, do you see for yourself in spousal spiritual direction? Discuss these with your spouse as you explore together how you might be able to implement at least some aspects of spiritual direction in your relationship. Consider talking with another couple about it and seeing what you might be able to do to encourage each other in such efforts.

Marriage is so intimate and personal that it would be wrong to closely pattern your friendship on what you see others experiencing. Nor should you expect to take what you read in a book—this or any book—and simply apply it. Each couple must work out a pattern of soul intimacy that fits them. This will be based on their personalities, histories, spiritual longings and a variety of other factors.

However, if anything in this chapter stirs your spirit, be bold enough to discuss it with your husband or wife. Take the risk of sharing your spiritual longings, for in doing so you share your spirit. Take the risk of sharing your apprehensions, for in doing so you share your soul. Take the risk of sharing your inner self, for in doing so you increase the possibilities of a genuine spiritual friendship.

Epilogue
The High Calling of Sacred Companions

There is no higher privilege than serving as a soul companion to others on the spiritual journey. In this act we are allowed to enter a truly holy place—the place where people meet with their God.

Accompanying others in a relationship of either spiritual friendship or direction allows us to share things that may have never been shared as fully with any other human being. Some people may share moments of epiphany and ecstasy as they encounter the Divine. Others may share agonizing doubt and despair as they encounter a glass ceiling that seems to block them from contact with their God. Both are equally sacred experiences.

Moses took off his shoes when he encountered the burning bush. He was in a sacred place—the presence of God. Metaphorically, I often feel a need to do likewise when talking with people about their spiritual journey. When I have this sense, I know that I have been blessed with spiritual discernment, for I have become aware of the presence of the Spirit.

This brings us back to the central theme of this book—attentiveness to the presence of God. Spiritual friends and directors ultimately face the same essential task. The essence of their role is discernment—or better, codiscernment. They, and those they accompany, seek to be attentive to the presence of the Flame That Does Not Consume.

The reason spiritual companionship is a sacred activity is that God saw fit to enter this role himself. As Jesus returned to heaven, he promised that he would send the Spirit to accompany God's people on the journey. This is why we call it a spiritual journey: it is a journey led by the Spirit. The Spirit is the form God's spiritual companionship takes. And the presence of the Spirit in this role in our lives and the lives of our spiritual friends is what makes our companionship sacred.

No one should seek to become a spiritual companion simply to meet his or her own needs. To do so is to have the focus on us rather than on God and the other person. One of the gifts of spiritual companionship is that we are blessed by the presence of the Spirit in the life of our friend, as well as in our friendship. Even in spiritual direction the director experiences rich spiritual blessings. But those blessings are not the primary reason for becoming a spiritual companion.

Our primary motive for becoming a spiritual companion should be love of others and desire to help them grow into the full measure of holiness and wholeness that is their eternal destiny. When love is the motive, our heart will be in the right place. When love is the motive, we are reminded that spiritual companions give themselves, not simply their advice or their expertise, to those they accompany. When love is the motive, we are reminded that anything of value that we give to others is grounded in God's love for us. That brings our attention back to the Great Lover of Souls—the One whose presence in our lives makes life worth living and whose presence in the lives of those we seek to accompany makes spiritual companionship sacred.

Suggestions for Further Reading

Resources listed in this annotated bibliography are selected as beginning points for further exploration of the issues addressed in this book. Some of these books are now out of print. However, you may still find them in used book stores, your church library or even some unexplored corner of your own home.

Books are first organized by category in order to help you find material related to specific interests. Full bibliographic information on each book is included in the General List, where books are arranged alphabetically by author.

Prayer

Bergan, Jacqueline, and S. Marie Schwan. *Love: A Guide for Prayer.*
Foster, Richard J. *Prayer: Finding the Heart's True Home.*
Green, Thomas. *When the Well Runs Dry.*
Hansen, David. *Long Wandering Prayer.*
Houston, James M. *The Transforming Power of Prayer.*
Keating, Thomas. *Open Mind, Open Heart.*
Nouwen, Henri. *The Way of the Heart.*
Pennington, Basil M. *Centering Prayer.*
Peterson, Eugene. *Answering God: The Psalms as Tools for Prayer.*

Lectio Divina

Casey, Michael. *Sacred Reading: The Ancient Art of Lectio Divina.*
Hall, Thelma. *Too Deep for Words: Rediscovering Lectio Divina.*
Vest, Norvene. *Gathered in the Word: Praying the Scripture in Small Groups.*

Meditation and Mysticism

Finley, James. *Merton's Palace of Nowhere.*
John of the Cross. *The Dark Night of the Soul.*
Keating, Thomas. *Open Mind, Open Heart.*
Main, John. *Moment of Christ: The Path of Meditation.*
May, Gerald. *Will and Spirit: A Contemplative Psychology.*

Merton, Thomas. *The Ascent to Truth.*
———. *New Seeds of Contemplation.*
Pennington, Basil M. *Centering Prayer.*
Rohr, Richard. *Everything Belongs.*
Teresa of Ávila. *Interior Castle.* Translated by E. A. Peers.
Underhill, Evelyn. *Practical Mysticism.*
Walsh, James, ed. *The Cloud of Unknowing.*

Soul Care
Benner, David G. *Care of Souls.*
Crabb, Larry. *The Safest Place on Earth.*
Edwards, Tilden. *Spiritual Friend.*
Gratton, Carolyn. *The Art of Spiritual Guidance.*
Jones, Alan. *Soul Making: The Desert Way of Spirituality.*
McNeill, John T. *A History of the Cure of Souls.*

Soul Friendship
Aelred of Rievaulx. *Spiritual Friendship.*
Crabb, Larry. *Connecting.*
Edwards, Tilden. *Spiritual Friend.*
Gratton, Carolyn. *The Art of Spiritual Guidance.*
Leech, Kenneth. *Soul Friend: The Practice of Christian Spirituality.*

Spiritual Direction
Anderson, Keith R., and Randy D. Reese. *Spiritual Mentoring.*
Bakke, Jeanette. *Holy Invitations.*
Barry, William. *Finding God in All Things.*
Barry, William, and William Connolly. *The Practice of
    Spiritual Direction.*
Chryssavgis, John. *Soul Mending.*
Edwards, Tilden. *Spiritual Friend.*
Gratton, Carolyn. *The Art of Spiritual Guidance.*
Guenther, Margaret. *Holy Listening.*
Ignatius. *The Spiritual Exercises.*
Leech, Kenneth. *Soul Friend.*
Luther, Martin. *Letters of Spiritual Counsel.* Translated by

Theodore Tappert.
Peterson, Eugene. *The Contemplative Pastor.*

Spiritual Biography and Autobiography

Augustine. *Confessions.* Translated by R. S. Pine-Coffin.
Chesterton, G. K. *St. Francis of Assisi.*
————. *St. Thomas Aquinas.*
Gaucher, Guy. *The Story of a Life: St. Thérèse of Lisieux.*
Green, Julien. *God's Fool: The Life and Times of Francis of Assisi.*
Merton, Thomas. *The Seven Story Mountain.*

Spiritual Theology

Alexander, Donald L., ed. *Christian Spirituality.*
Chan, Simon. *Spiritual Theology.*
John of the Cross. *The Dark Night of the Soul.*
Leech, Kenneth. *Experiencing God: Theology as Spirituality.*
Lovelace, Richard. *Dynamics of Spiritual Life.*
Merton, Thomas. *The Ascent to Truth.*
Teresa of Ávila. *Interior Castle.* Translated by E. A. Peers.

Spiritual Dynamics and Formation

Barry, William. *Finding God in All Things.*
Bernard of Clairvaux. *Selected Works.* Translated by G. R. Evans.
Bonhoeffer, Dietrich. *The Cost of Discipleship.*
Chester, Michael P., and Marie C. Norrisey. *Prayer and Temperament.*
Crabb, Larry. *Shattered Dreams.*
Fénelon, François. *Christian Perfection.*
Finley, James. *Merton's Palace of Nowhere.*
Foster, Richard J. *Celebration of Discipline.*
————. *Streams of Living Water.*
Francis de Sales. *Introduction to the Devout Life.*
Francis of Assisi. *The Little Flowers of St. Francis.*
Gorsuch, John P. *An Invitation to the Spiritual Journey.*
Green, Thomas H. *A Vacation with the Lord.*
Hudson, Trevor. *Christ Following: Ten Signposts to Spirituality.*
John of the Cross. *The Dark Night of the Soul.*

Jones, Alan. *Soul Making: The Desert Way of Spirituality.*
Kierkegaard, Søren. *Purity of Heart.* Translated by D. V. Steere.
Merton, Thomas. *New Seeds of Contemplation.*
Moon, Gary. *Homesick for Eden.*
Mulholland, M. Robert. *Invitation to a Journey.*
———. *Shaped by the Word.*
Norris, Kathleen. *The Cloister Walk.*
Nouwen, Henri. *The Inner Voice of Love.*
———. *Reaching Out.*
———. *The Return of the Prodigal Son.*
———. *The Way of the Heart.*
Packer, J. I. *Quest for Godliness.*
Pennington, Basil M. *Living in the Question.*
———. *True Self/False Self.*
Rohr, Richard. *Everything Belongs.*
Santa-Maria, Maria. *Growth Through Meditation and Journal Writing.*
Savary, Louis, Patricia Berne and Strephon Williams. *Dreams and Spiritual Growth.*
Sproul, R. C. *The Holiness of God.*
Tan, Siang-Yang, and Douglas Gregg. *Disciplines of the Holy Spirit.*
Teresa of Ávila. *Interior Castle.* Translated by E. A. Peers.
Thomas à Kempis. *The Imitation of Christ.*
Tozer, A. W. *The Knowledge of the Holy.*
Van Kaam, Adrian. *On Being Yourself.*
Ware, Corinne. *Discover Your Spiritual Type.*
Wesley, John. *A Plain Account of Christian Perfection.*
Willard, Dallas. *The Divine Conspiracy.*

Retreat Resources
Barry, William. *Finding God in All Things.*
Bergan, Jacqueline, and S. Marie Schwan. *Love: A Guide for Prayer.*
Chester, Michael P., and Marie C. Norrisey. *Prayer and Temperament.*
Green, Thomas H. *A Vacation with the Lord.*
Griffin, Emilie. *Wilderness Time: A Guide for Spiritual Retreat.*
Ignatius. *The Spiritual Exercises.*
Jones, Timothy. *A Place for God.*

Laubach, Frank. *Practicing His Presence.*

Law, William. *A Serious Call to the Devout and Holy Life.*

Lawrence, Brother. *The Practice of the Presence of God.*

Nouwen, Henri. *The Return of the Prodigal Son.*

Retreats Online <www.retreatsonline.com>.

Smith, James, and Lynda Graybeal. *A Spiritual Formation Workbook.*

Vennard, Jane E. *Be Still: Designing and Leading Contemplative Retreats.*

Ware, Corinne. *Discover Your Spiritual Type.*

Psychological Dynamics and Formation

Brenner, Charles. *An Elementary Textbook of Psychoanalysis.*

Fowler, James. *Stages of Faith.*

Freud, Anna. *The Ego and the Mechanisms of Defense.*

Freud, Sigmund. *Introductory Lectures on Psychoanalysis.*

Fromm, Erich. *The Art of Loving.*

———. *The Meaning of Anxiety.*

James, William. *The Varieties of Religious Experience.*

Keirsey, David, and Marilyn Bates. *Please Understand Me.*

Kunkle, Fritz. *Selected Writings.* Edited by John Sanford.

Laing, R. D. *The Divided Self.*

Lake, Frank. *Clinical Theology.*

Lewis, C. S. *The Four Loves.*

Loder, James. *The Transforming Moment.*

May, Gerald. *Addiction and Grace.*

———. *Will and Spirit: A Contemplative Psychology.*

Narramore, Bruce. *No Condemnation.*

O'Donohue, John. *Eternal Echoes.*

Peck, M. Scott. *People of the Lie.*

Riso, Don Richard. *Personality Types.*

———. *Understanding the Enneagram.*

Shapiro, David. *Neurotic Styles.*

Sugerman, Shirley. *Sin and Madness: Studies in Narcissism.*

Tournier, Paul. *Guilt and Grace.*

———. *The Meaning of Persons.*

———. *A Place for You.*

Vanier, Jean. *Becoming Human.*

General Listing

Aelred of Rievaulx. *Spiritual Friendship.* Kalamazoo, Mich.: Cistercian, 1977. Written by a twelfth-century monk who has come to be the unofficial patron saint of spiritual directors, this book presents a timeless discussion of friendship and its role in spiritual direction. It remains one of the richest discussions of spiritual friendship—emphasizing its importance for any genuine spiritual growth, recognizing its demands and complexities, and honoring the gift that it always represents.

Alexander, Donald L., ed. *Christian Spirituality: Five Views of Sanctification.* Downers Grove, Ill.: InterVarsity Press, 1988. This comparison of five major contemporary Christian spiritual traditions—Reformed, Lutheran, Wesleyan, Pentecostal and contemplative—provides a helpful exploration of the theological foundations of each. Its emphasis is on the explicit and implicit understanding of sanctification that undergirds each of the spiritual traditions. Its major contribution is the help it provides in grounding spirituality in theology. Those interested in comparative Protestant spiritualities will find it most beneficial.

Anderson, Keith R., and Randy D. Reese. *Spiritual Mentoring: A Guide for Seeking and Giving Direction.* Downers Grove, Ill.: InterVarsity Press, 1999. Describing spiritual mentoring in terms that are quite similar to the understanding of spiritual direction presented here, this book provides a helpful discussion of accompaniment on the spiritual journey.

Augustine. *Confessions.* Translated by R. S. Pine-Coffin. New York: Penguin, 1961. This book by St. Augustine of Hippo from the fourth century A.D. remains one of the classics of Western literature in general and

Christian spirituality in particular. It presents an unsurpassed personal account of the spiritual journey of a great sinner who became a great saint, offering an intimate examination of his experience in the light of Scripture and the leading of the Holy Spirit.

Bakke, Jeanette. *Holy Invitations: Exploring Spiritual Direction.* Grand Rapids, Mich.: Baker, 2000. This book presents a thorough and extremely helpful introduction to spiritual direction from an evangelical point of view. Even more, it serves as a wonderful discussion of how to listen to your heart and to God.

Barry, William A. *Finding God in All Things: A Companion to the Spiritual Exercises of St. Ignatius.* Notre Dame, Ind.: Ave Maria, 1991. This is one of the most helpful contemporary discussions of the core spiritual dynamics of the Ignatian spiritual exercises that I have found. It presents a fresh and engaging presentation of what it means to find God in everyday life—a central feature of the Ignatian approach to Christian spirituality. Not only personally edifying, it is also of great value to those seeking to offer spiritual direction or lead spiritual growth retreats.

Barry, William A., and William J. Connolly. *The Practice of Spiritual Direction.* San Francisco: Harper & Row, 1982. This has rapidly become something like the standard modern textbook on spiritual direction. Highly practical, biblically grounded and clearly written, it offers help for anyone seeking to offer spiritual direction or better understand what is involved in doing so.

Benner, David G. *Care of Souls: Revisioning Christian Nurture and Counsel.* Grand Rapids, Mich.: Baker, 1998. Describing the soul as the meeting point of the psychological and spiritual aspects of persons, this book seeks to reunite these strands of personhood by the recovery of soul care as a central ministry of the church. After a review of the history and distinctives of Christian soul care, it sets out the contours of a psychologically grounded vision of Christian spirituality and suggests how the inner nature of persons can be nurtured by means of a variety of relationships of care. Somewhat more theoretical than the present book, it also offers practical discussion of such topics as how to listen in soul care dialogue, working with dreams in supporting spiritual growth, how to prepare for and best use a relationship of soul care, and the care of one's own soul.

Bergan, Jacqueline, and S. Marie Schwan. *Love: A Guide for Prayer.* Winona, Minn.: St. Mary's, 1985. This is a book for prayer, not about prayer. The first of a five-book series, it serves as an excellent resource for either personal or shared prayer in a spiritual accompaniment group or a contemplative retreat. Based on the Ignatian spiritual exercises, it offers six weeks of daily meditations on biblical passages related to the Exercises' first theme—knowing God's love. An introductory chapter helpfully discusses meditation, contemplation, centering prayer and other forms of prayer. The daily meditations then present suggestions for possible prayer responses to each biblical passage. It, and the entire series it introduces, will be richly appreciated by anyone hungering to know God more deeply.

Bernard of Clairvaux. *Selected Works.* Translated by G. R. Evans. New York: Paulist, 1988. This book presents a selection of Bernard's most important contributions to the understanding of growth in intimacy with God. His focus is on what it means to grow in love, particularly in the love of God. Bernard describes four stages in this process, noting that God's love of us is both the prime mover of our love and the final end. Filled with psychologically and spiritually astute observations, this book deserves its status as a classic of Christian spirituality.

Bonhoeffer, Dietrich. *The Cost of Discipleship.* New York: Macmillan, 1963. Written by a German Lutheran pastor whose discipleship eventually cost him his life, this book offers a powerful encounter with Christ's call to follow him. Addressing the questions "What did Jesus mean to say to us?" and "What is his will for us today?" Bonhoeffer's answers are rooted in Scripture (almost a third of the book consisting of an extended meditation on the Sermon on the Mount) and emphasize grace. He contrasts "cheap grace" and "costly grace." Cheap grace, he notes, is what we bestow on ourselves; it omits discipleship. In contrast, costly grace "costs a man his life . . . [but] is grace because it gives a man the only true life."

Brenner, Charles. *An Elementary Textbook of Psychoanalysis.* Garden City, N.Y.: Doubleday, 1974. This small paperback presents the most comprehensive and readable overview of psychoanalytic theory available for the layperson. An excellent companion to Sigmund Freud's *Introductory Lectures on Psychoanalysis,* it explains and organizes all the major aspects of this complex and often somewhat daunting theory, making clear why Freud's insights remain so important for any contemporary depth psychology, and indeed for any comprehensive understanding of the dynamics of the soul.

Casey, Michael. *Sacred Reading: The Ancient Art of Lectio Divina.* New York: Triumph, 1996. This is another wonderful discussion of the ancient form of prayerful listening to Scripture, setting the practice within the Benedictine tradition and providing good coverage of its theological roots as well as its practical applications.

Chan, Simon. *Spiritual Theology: A Systematic Study of the Christian Life*. Downers Grove, Ill.: InterVarsity Press, 1998. If you can read only one book on spiritual theology and you want it to be both solidly evangelical and broadly ecumenical, this is the book for you. It provides an excellent discussion of the theological foundation of spirituality, as well as the major forms of practice of the spiritual life that have evolved over time in the Christian church.

Chester, Michael P., and Marie C. Norrisey. *Prayer and Temperament: Different Prayer Forms for Different Personality Types*. Charlottesville, Va.: Open Door, 1984. This book does a good job of relating personality types (as measured by the Myers-Briggs personality classification) and forms of prayer. Its greatest contribution is not simply identifying prayer forms that fit personality types but encouraging the reader to explore other ways of experiencing God. Doing so helps one appreciate other spiritual styles and also promotes personal growth. The book contains an appendix that lets you determine your own personality type.

Chesterton, G. K. *St. Thomas Aquinas*. New York: Image, 1974. Widely regarded as one of the best books ever written on St. Thomas, this is Chesterton at his best. This classic portrait of a great and influential Christian theologian is accessible and engaging—a wonderful spiritual biography.

———. *St. Francis of Assisi*. New York: Image, 1987. Chesterton, one of the great Christian writers and thinkers of the twentieth century, converted to Roman Catholicism in 1922 because, he reportedly said, "only the Roman Church could produce a St. Francis of Assisi." Published shortly after his conversion, this book is one of the finest biographies of St. Francis.

Chryssavgis, John. *Soul Mending: The Art of Spiritual Direction*. Brookline, Mass.: Holy Cross Orthodox, 2000. This is an eminently wise book on spiritual direction from the perspective of Eastern Orthodoxy. With an appendix that provides seventy-five pages of summaries of the most important patristic sources on spiritual direction, this resource will be appreciated by all who seek to better understand the rich contributions to the understanding of spiritual direction that have come from the Orthodox Church.

The Cloud of Unknowing. Edited by James Walsh. New York: Paulist, 1981. Written by an anonymous fourteenth-century English monk, this book presents the meat of advanced Christian meditation for those who have already drunk of the milk and desired more. It describes a method of contemplation that emphasizes the limitations of understanding as we seek to break through the cloud of unknowing that separates God and humans. Although Protestants often are troubled by the emphasis on the incomprehensibility of God associated with what is known as the apophatic tradition in Christian meditation, it does serve as a helpful counterbalance to the tendency to a familiarity with God that leads to an elimination of mystery.

Crabb, Larry. *Connecting.* Nashville: Word, 1997. This book explores the implications of the author's observation that "when people connect . . . something is poured out of one and into the other that has the power to heal the soul of its deepest wounds and restore it to health." Have no doubt about it, the implications of such connections are immense. Here popular author and psychologist Crabb explores the power of spiritual communities—a power sufficient, he argues, to heal us of the soul diseases that keep us from wholeness.

———. *The Safest Place on Earth.* Nashville: Word, 1999. Spiritual communities hold potential for personal transformation that are seldom actualized in churches as they typically exist. This book is not, however, a critique of the church. Rather, it sets out a stirring vision of what can happen when Christians form genuine spiritual communities. Including rich discussion of both spiritual friends and spiritual directors, this book is a wonderful resource not only for one's own journey but particularly for those who seek to accompany others as soul friends and guides.

———. *Shattered Dreams.* Colorado Springs: WaterBrook, 2001. This book presents a powerful vision of encountering God in the midst of life's most difficult circumstances. Built around the story of Naomi in the book of Ruth, it describes the basis for the hope of both transformation and joy as a result of daring to meet the Spirit in the midst of our pain.

Edwards, Tilden. *Spiritual Friend: Reclaiming the Gift of Spiritual Direction.* New York: Paulist, 1980. Divided into two parts, this book first explores the historic Christian heritage of spiritual direction and then offers a detailed discussion of how to find a spiritual friend and be one for others. The second, more practical half of the book contains a helpful chapter on group direction that positions such groups very close to the spiritual accompaniment groups I have described.

Fénelon, François. *Christian Perfection.* Translated by Mildred Stillman. New York: Harper, 1947. Here are forty-one short meditations (drawn from the author's letters of spiritual counsel) on a range of topics related to Christian spirituality. The book is devotional in spirit and should be read slowly and meditatively. It is a treasury of wisdom from a man whose love of his Lord is deep and obvious, and whose skill in guiding others on the Christian spiritual journey has given him a place of esteem among Christian spiritual directors since these meditations were first written three hundred years ago.

Finley, James. *Merton's Palace of Nowhere: A Search for God Through Awareness of the True Self.* Notre Dame, Ind.: Ave Maria, 1978. Neither the title nor the subtitle adequately captures the focus of this rich and at times profound book. Finely was a fellow monk in the Abbey of Gethsemani with Thomas Merton before he left the order and became a clinical psychologist. His modesty leads him to suggest that what he offers in this book is reflections on the insights of Merton. But this is much more than reflections on someone else's ideas. It is an original and important contribution to the understanding of Christian spiritual formation, particularly those aspects that deal with freedom from the tyranny of our self-deceptions and delusions.

Foster, Richard J. *Celebration of Discipline: The Path to Spiritual Growth.* San Francisco: Harper & Row, 1978, rev. ed. HarperSanFrancisco, 1998. For over twenty years this book has provided a wonderful introduction to the classic disciplines of Christian spirituality. Organized around thirteen spiritual practices that have been foundational to Christian spiritual formation, it offers enormous help to those who seek to understand and advance in the spiritual journey.

————. *Prayer: Finding the Heart's True Home.* San Francisco: HarperSanFrancisco, 1992. This book offers rich resources for anyone seeking to deepen their engagement with God through prayer. Exploring diverse aspects and forms such as prayer of adoration and rest, sacramental prayer, meditation and contemplation, it speaks to both head and heart. Read prayerfully, this book will transform your prayer life.

————. *Streams of Living Water: Celebrating the Great Traditions of Christian Faith.* San Francisco: HarperSanFrancisco, 1998. This book presents a history of Christian spirituality, exploring what the author identifies as the six major traditions of Christian life and faith—contemplative, holiness, charismatic, social justice, evangelical and incarnational. Foster's approach is not academic or scholarly but personal, spiritual and transformational as he seeks to identify what can be taken from each tradition in supporting a balanced, full-orbed contemporary spirituality. This excellent book forms the foundation for many of the other titles by Foster and his colleagues published in the Renovaré Resources for Spiritual Renewal series of HarperSanFrancisco.

Fowler, James. *Stages of Faith.* San Francisco: HarperSanFrancisco, 1981. Fowler presents pioneering work on the nature and development of faith. His approach is broad, not assuming that faith is necessarily religious or associated with belief. Rather, faith is the way of making sense of life. Numerous Christian authors have built on Fowler's framework in attempts to understand the specifics of Christian faith development, but the source of their inspiration remains worth studying.

Francis de Sales. *Introduction to the Devout Life.* Translated by J. K. Ryan. New York: Doubleday, 1955. Written as a letter to a person desiring growth in love of God, this spiritual classic presents invaluable advice for the Christian transformational journey. Although the language reflects the author's seventeenth-century French Roman Catholic context, the spirit of these meditations transcends culture and time. They reveal a wise but humble spiritual director whose love for the Lord is obvious and whose understanding of spiritual formation is profound.

Francis of Assisi. *The Little Flowers of St. Francis.* Translated by E. M. Blaiklock and A. C. Keys. Ann Arbor, Mich.: Servant, 1985. This book provides an engaging encounter with the sayings and deeds of the twelfth-century saint Francis of Assisi. His compassion for the poor and sick, his disregard for material possessions and his single-minded passion for God make him a truly remarkable man. His story has inspired Christians from every tradition for as long as it has been told, and there is no better introduction to that story than this little book.

Freud, Anna. *The Ego and the Mechanisms of Defense.* New York: International Universities Press, 1966. Written by the daughter of the founder of psychoanalysis, this book represents an excellent discussion of the mental defense mechanisms. An understanding of these ways in which we unconsciously seek to defend against anxiety by distorting reality form one of the most important contributions of psychoanalysis. Amply illustrated with cases drawn from the author's practice with children, this book also serves as an extremely valuable contribution to child psychology, particularly the nature of unconscious conflict in children and adolescents.

Freud, Sigmund. *Introductory Lectures on Psychoanalysis.* Translated by James Strachey. New York: W. W. Norton, 1966. This is perhaps the best available introduction to the writings of Sigmund Freud, whose insights remain indispensable to any comprehensive understanding of the dynamics of the soul. The lectures display Freud's gift for exposition at its height; most readers discover that he is considerably easier to read than to read about. The book contains a good overview of his theory of dreams as well as his understanding of anxiety, neurotic conflict and psychoanalytic therapy.

Fromm, Erich. *The Art of Loving.* New York: Harper & Row, 1956. This small book serves as an excellent companion to *The Four Loves* by C. S. Lewis in its contributions to understanding the nature of love. Sales of millions of copies have kept it a bestseller in numerous languages around the world, and the reason is the author's simple but profound understanding of the challenges of love and his daring call for us to commit ourselves to it.

———. *The Meaning of Anxiety.* New York: Simon & Schuster, 1950. Here Fromm presents anxiety not as a symptom to be eliminated but as a messenger from the depths of our soul to be received with gratitude. The essential nature of anxiety and its crucial role in authentic living are presented with clarity and conviction in a book that is, from my point of view, the author's most important work.

Gaucher, Guy. *The Story of a Life: St. Thérèse of Lisieux.* San Francisco: Harper & Row, 1987. During her short life nothing much about Thérèse of Lisieux was remarkable. She was misunderstood by her fellow nuns, who perceived her as being neglectful of her duties, and even her passionate love of Jesus was scarcely recognized by others. But her death at age twenty-four allowed others to see into her soul as it opened her notebooks, letters, poems and written prayers to the world. Quickly the depth of her devotion and spiritual maturity became apparent, and she gained a following around the world through her writings. This biography lets her speak with her own voice. Based entirely on her own words, it allows us to encounter this young French girl who loved God with all her heart and soul. Doing so is a spiritual privilege.

Gorsuch, John P. *An Invitation to the Spiritual Journey.* New York: Paulist, 1990. This little book sparkles. Written with a light touch, it reads as a series of meditations on nine dimensions of the Christian spiritual journey. Saturated with the wisdom of Christian spiritual writers who have gone before, it speaks directly and engagingly to those who seek to know God more deeply and allow their lives to be transformed by that knowing.

Gratton, Carolyn. *The Art of Spiritual Guidance.* New York: Crossroad, 1993. Reading this book takes a little work. However, this will be repaid with ample dividends of profound insight regarding the dynamics of Christian spiritual formation and the process of spiritual direction. The author, an experienced psychologist and spiritual director, is ecumenical in her approach, and her use of nonconventional names of God may be a bit off-putting for some readers. However, the book is one of the best sources available on Christian spiritual formation and direction, and I recommend it highly.

Green, Julien. *God's Fool: The Life and Times of Francis of Assisi.* San Francisco: Harper & Row, 1983. This biography of Francis of Assisi places him within the context of his times and brings this most remarkable Christian to life. It is a nonsentimental account of his life, his conversion and his effect on the medieval church of France. Through it we too can encounter "God's fool"—a man through whom the face of the church and the world has been changed.

Green, Thomas H. *A Vacation with the Lord.* Notre Dame, Ind.: Ave Maria, 1986. Based on the Ignatian spiritual exercises, this book presents the framework for an eight-day spiritual retreat. I have used this several times for personal retreats, have guided others through it and recommend it highly. Although not its primary purpose, it also serves as an excellent introduction to the Ignatian spiritual exercises.

————. *When the Well Runs Dry: Prayer Beyond the Beginnings.* Notre Dame, Ind.: Ave Maria, 1998. This book is a rich source of guidance for those serious about prayer and ready for advanced instruction. Drawing richly on the wisdom of Teresa of Ávila, John of the Cross and Ignatius of Loyola, it offers wise guidance in the face of the "dark nights of the soul" that are inevitably a part of a life of prayer. If you want to move beyond Prayer 101, this is one of the best texts to help you do so.

Griffin, Emilie. *Wilderness Time: A Guide for Spiritual Retreat.* San Francisco: HarperSanFrancisco, 1997. One of the signs of a new interest in spirituality among Protestants is the rise in interest in the ancient Christian practice of retreats. This book serves as an excellent introduction to the use of retreats in spiritual formation and provides encouragement and practical help in designing your own personal retreat. It is also highly relevant to those who seek to lead others on retreats.

Guenther, Margaret. *Holy Listening: The Art of Spiritual Direction.* Boston: Cowley, 1992. This warm and wise book is full of helpful insights on spiritual direction. Building on an understanding of the process that emphasizes presence and attentiveness, the author brings a woman's perspective to holy listening. The book is of great value to both men and women seeking to serve as spiritual directors or friends.

Hall, Thelma. *Too Deep for Words: Rediscovering Lectio Divina*. New York: Paulist, 1988. This book provides a very good introduction to this ancient form of prayer, reviewing its history and presenting a method for its practice. Particularly helpful is a thematically organized list of passages of Scripture most suitable for this form of meditative reading.

Hansen, David. *Long Wandering Prayer: An Invitation to Walk with God.* Downers Grove, Ill.: InterVarsity Press, 2001. In this book I discovered that I am not alone in finding my deepest experiences of prayer as I walk. The author of this engaging and wonderful discussion of prayer encourages the reader to use the fact that our minds wander as an advantage to prayer rather than a disadvantage. I strongly recommend it if you seek to find God in the spaces of your life and learn to walk with him.

Houston, James M. *The Transforming Power of Prayer: Deepening Your Friendship with God.* Colorado Springs: NavPress, 1999. This book describes prayer as friendship with God, not simply a spiritual discipline or skill to be mastered. The author's own obvious divine friendship makes this a work that sparkles. It has the potential to transform your prayer and your own friendship with God.

Hudson, Trevor. *Christ Following: Ten Signposts to Spirituality.* Grand Rapids, Mich.: Revell, 1996. Drawing from classical spiritual writings as well as his experience as a pastor in South Africa, Trevor Hudson describes ten disciplines for developing a passion for Christ. A powerful, wise and at times absolutely profound little book that will be richly appreciated by anyone serious about Christ following.

Ignatius. *The Spiritual Exercises.* Translated by Louis J. Puhl. Manila: Society of St. Paul, 1990. This is one of several recent translations of the classic set of spiritual meditations developed by St. Ignatius and forming the best-known framework for a spiritual retreat developed in the history of the Christian church. Written for spiritual directors, it is not suitable for a self-guided retreat. However, it will be helpful to those who seek to better understand the Ignatian approach to spiritual formation and direction.

James, William. *The Varieties of Religious Experience.* New York: Collier, 1961. This book stands as one of the classics of the field of the psychology of religion. The author, a noted philosopher and psychologist, argues that evidence for God lies primarily in personal experience rather than in abstract philosophical arguments. The book is an excel-

lent introduction to the psychological study of religious experience. Its
review of the effects of religious faith on personality is particularly helpful, even if challenging when James describes the ways religion frequently supports both healthy and unhealthy dynamics.

John of the Cross. *The Dark Night of the Soul.* Translated by E. Allison
Peers. New York: Doubleday/Image, 1990. The phrase "the dark night of
the soul" has come to stand for spiritual dryness or a sense of being
abandoned by God. This is the book that gave us that phrase. Here the
sixteenth-century Spanish mystic St. John of the Cross notes the inevi-
tability of dark nights on the Christian spiritual journey. More important, however, he suggests the way they can lead us to perfect love of
God. The little book isn't always easy to read, understand or apply. But
it remains a classic of Christian spirituality because of the wisdom of
the psychological and spiritual insights it communicates.

Jones, Alan. *Soul Making: The Desert Way of Spirituality.* San Francisco:
Harper & Row, 1985. In the preface the author describes this book as
being "about how humans being are made." "Soul making," an ancient
metaphor for this, reminds us that personal formation starts on the
inside, not the outside. Focusing on love as the crucible of soul making,
Jones identifies foundational elements of the spirituality of the fourth-
century desert fathers and argues for their importance in the lives of
contemporary Christians. This book is for anyone spiritually hungry
and open to learn from Christian traditions other than his or her own.

Jones, Timothy. *A Place for God: A Guide to Spiritual Retreats and Retreat
Churches.* New York: Doubleday, 2000. Listing over 250 retreat centers
in Canada and the United States, this book is a helpful resource to those
seeking a retreat center. It also contains a helpful discussion of how to
prepare for a retreat and how best to use the experience.

Keating, Thomas. *Open Mind, Open Heart: The Contemplative Dimension
of the Gospel.* New York: Continuum, 1994. This is probably the best
introduction to centering prayer that exists. Keating presents it as a distinctively Christian form of meditation, briefly exploring its origins in
the ancient church and then demonstrating its use as "a sign of one's
intention" to surrender to God. Centering prayer is a discipline of rest-
ing in God's presence. It offers a powerful antidote to the compulsive
busyness that leaves many Christians spiritually shallow and frustrated.

Keirsey, David, and Marilyn Bates. *Please Understand Me: Character and
Temperament Types.* New York: Prometheus, 1984. For those unfamiliar

with the Myers-Briggs type indicator, this book provides an excellent introduction to this now-classic personality typology and assessment tool. It also includes a very helpful seventy-question "Keirsey Temperament Sorter," a sort of mini-Myers-Briggs test that places you in one of sixteen personality types.

Kierkegaard, Søren. *Purity of Heart.* Translated by D. V. Steere. New York: Harper & Row, 1956. Noting that it is the pure in heart who will see God, this examination of inner purity is written with passion and exudes the intimate experience of the author with his subject. His short answer to the question of just what purity of heart is: to will one thing, the good that God wills.

Kunkle, Fritz. *Selected Writings.* Edited by John Sanford. New York: Ramsey, 1984. This collection of writings serves as an excellent introduction to the work of one of the least-known pioneers of modern depth psychology. Fritz Kunkle is particularly relevant to Christians, not only because he was a devout Christian but also because his writings reflect his lifelong desire to develop a comprehensive religious psychology. This selection contains portions of his two most important books, *How Character Develops* and *In Search of Maturity.* The central theme of the book is egocentricity. The author's discussion of how it develops, how it sets us up for an inevitable crisis (often at midlife), and the route through this crisis makes an important contribution to an understanding of the dynamics of the soul.

Laing, R. D. *The Divided Self.* New York: Penguin, 1965. This book became something of a cult classic on university campuses in the 1970s. Its purpose is exploration of the nature and meaning of madness, particularly as it appears in schizophrenia. Its popular appeal reflects the fact that it is far from a dry clinical treatment of the subject, exploring instead the phenomenology, or experience, of madness. Four decades after its original publication it remains a valuable contribution to the understanding of the fragmentation of the human mind; it also serves as a good introduction to the existential approach to psychology.

Lake, Frank. *Clinical Theology.* London: Darton, Longman & Todd, 1986. This is an abridged edition of a work that, while somewhat obscure, makes an important contribution to an understanding of the spiritual and psychological basis of psychopathology and its cure. Insights about the nature of depression, hysteria, paranoia and the schizoid style reveal the author's grounding in the object relations psychoanalytic tradition. Written for clergy and laity, the book does require some familiarity with depth psychology, although a patient, careful reading will go a long way to providing just that.

Laubach, Frank. *Practicing His Presence*. Goleta, Calif.: Christian Books, 1976. Written by a twentieth-century missionary in the Philippines, this book is a modern-day sequel to Brother Lawrence's *The Practice of the Presence of God*. In January 1930 Laubach began the discipline of turning his mind to Christ one second out of every minute of his waking day. The result was transforming. This is a powerful account of one man's experience of the renewal of the mind that comes from attunement to the presence of God.

Law, William. *A Serious Call to the Devout and Holy Life*. Nashville: Upper Room, 1952. This book presents an eighteenth-century English Puritan account of the spiritual life in a manner that speaks to Christians in any century, country or denomination who seek to grow in holiness. It reminds the reader of the high standards of holiness in a way that encourages rather than discourages the pursuit of God.

Lawrence, Brother. *The Practice of the Presence of God*. New York: Harper & Row, 1941. Brother Lawrence was a humble seventeenth-century lay brother in a monastery who set out to learn how to pray without ceasing. While washing dishes he learned to cultivate the presence of God so completely that he could joyfully exclaim, "I am doing now what I will do for all eternity. I am blessing God, praising Him, adoring Him, and loving Him with all my heart." In fewer than a hundred short pages of text, this book introduces you to a gentle and humble Christian who has much to teach about the secret of attuning our souls to God.

Leech, Kenneth. *Experiencing God: Theology as Spirituality*. San Francisco: Harper & Row, 1985. This is an excellent contemporary introduction to a theology of spirituality. It examines the major ways God has been experienced from Old Testament times to the present. The result is a comprehensive overview of Christian spirituality, including the major traditions within it.

———. *Soul Friend: The Practice of Christian Spirituality*. New York: Harper & Row, 1980. This book is a good introduction to spiritual direction, with particularly helpful coverage of its history. It also presents a useful discussion of differences between spiritual direction and both counseling and psychotherapy. It is at its best, however, in two chapters devoted to prayer. These review approaches to prayer in the major

Christian traditions across church history and present an excellent discussion of forms of prayer and the role of silence in prayer.

Lewis, C. S. *The Four Loves*. London: Fontana, 1960. Distinguishing four forms of love—eros, charity, affection and friendship—this book presents a helpful discussion of how each differs from and yet relates to the others. The examination of friendship is particularly valuable, as is the way Lewis places each of the forms of love within a Christian understanding.

Loder, James. *The Transforming Moment: Understanding Convictional Experiences*. New York: Harper & Row, 1981. This book seeks to articulate the relationship between the human spirit and the Holy Spirit in a way that is informed by developmental and psychoanalytic psychology. It is an exceptionally fine discussion of Christian spiritual formation that integrates the theoretical and practical aspects of the topic. It is, however, for the serious reader and requires some background in both psychology and theology.

Lovelace, Richard. *Dynamics of Spiritual Life*. Downers Grove, Ill.: Inter-Varsity Press, 1979. The author describes this book as a manual of spiritual theology. After examining the history of spiritual renewals and a range of biblical models of revival, it sets out a comprehensive framework for personal and congregational renewal. Grounded in the evangelical tradition, it presents a theology of spiritual renewal that is of value far beyond the tradition out of which it developed.

Luther, Martin. *Letters of Spiritual Counsel*. Translated by Theodore Tappert. Philadelphia: Westminster Press, 1955. This is perhaps the classic Protestant account of the use of correspondence as a means of providing spiritual direction. Showing the pastoral heart of this great theologian, it wonderfully illustrates this intimate nature of pastoral care that is directed toward spiritual formation.

Main, John. *Moment of Christ: The Path of Meditation*. New York: Crossroad, 1986. This book presents a rich and engaging discussion of Christian meditation. In a series of short devotional reflections on topics related to stillness of heart and a focus on God, the underlying theme is the reminder that prayer consists of being swept into the presence of Christ. The book is, in fact, just such a prayer.

May, Gerald. *Addiction and Grace*. San Francisco: HarperSanFrancisco, 1991. This book examines the variety of addictions from which we can suffer and describes spiritual responses that hold promise for their resolution. The author argues that our attachments prevent us from responding to God's grace and gain their power through the same biological mechanism as addictions to substances. The result is a discussion of the dynamics of addiction that interweaves psychological and spiritual dimensions in a helpful manner.

————. *Will and Spirit: A Contemplative Psychology.* San Francisco: Harper & Row, 1983. Written by a psychiatrist and Christian spiritual director, this book presents the first fruits of May's attempt to build a psychology on an exploration of human consciousness guided by the resources of ancient Christian contemplative wisdom. At the core of the book is his discussion of the profound difference between two postures toward life—willingness and willfulness. Exploring the spiritual significance of these postures, he develops the implications for a psychology of fear, love, conflict, evil and a number of other aspects of human functioning. The book assumes no background in either psychology or contemplative spirituality, although openness to the latter will serve to make May's approach more intelligible and the results of more interest. This is a book I return to time and time again.

McColman, Carl. *Spirituality: Where Body and Soul Encounter the Sacred.* Georgetown, Mass.: North Star, 1997. Written from an ecumenical Christian perspective, this work is theologically less orthodox than most others included in these readings. Its value lies in the understanding of spirituality that the author presents. Don't read it if you strongly prefer books that support how you already understand things. But if you are interested in allowing interfaith dialogue to interact with a Christian understanding of spirituality, this book will serve you well.

McNeill, John T. *A History of the Cure of Souls.* New York: Harper & Row, 1951. This book presents a panoramic review of the patterns of soul care that have been present in each age of the church across its history. It is helpful for understanding the rich variety of ways in which people have structured relationships of spiritual nurture and soul friendship.

Merton, Thomas. *The Ascent to Truth.* San Diego: Harcourt Brace, 1951. Be forewarned. This is the meat of mystical and spiritual theology. But it is probably Merton's most profound work on the nature of Christian mysticism, particularly as expressed in the sixteenth-century Spanish saint John of the Cross. If you wish to understand Christian mysticism, and in particular seek to understand better the way through what Merton calls "the darkness that can only be enlightened by the fire of love," this is a book you will treasure for the rest of your life.

————. *New Seeds of Contemplation.* New York: New Directions, 1961.

Although many people find Merton difficult to understand, he remains my personal favorite of all the spiritual authors in this listing. And this is my favorite of all his books. In my judgment it presents his clearest discussion of the nature of the false self, its relation to sin and the process of becoming our true self-in-Christ. Thirty-nine short chapters also give rich insights on other matters such as the role of solitude in spiritual development, the nature of faith, the mystery of life in Christ, the dynamics of love of God and the nature of contemplative prayer. Combing psychological insights with the deep knowledge of the spiritual journey that comes from an acknowledged master in understanding and describing that journey, this is psychospiritual theory and practice at its very best!

————. *The Seven Story Mountain.* San Diego: Harcourt Brace Jovanovich, 1948. Hailed as a twentieth-century masterpiece equivalent in importance to *The Confessions of St. Augustine*, this is the autobiography of a modern saint—Thomas Merton. It is the account of a young man's spiritual journey from atheism and religious disinterest, through a growing spiritual restlessness, to a dramatic religious conversion followed quickly by a call to the priesthood and subsequent entry to a Trappist monastery—what he called the "four walls of my new freedom." It reads with sparkle and wit but is more than an engaging story or great literature. It is a spiritual odyssey that tells the remarkable story of the formation and transformation of a modern soul.

Moon, Gary. *Homesick for Eden.* Franklin Springs, Ga.: LifeSprings, 1996. This is a book that will at once gratify spiritual hunger and stimulate it. The author writes with a fresh and clear style, and the book has a personal and engaging voice. In allegorical form, this brilliant little book's images will touch your soul and rekindle its longing to return home. Do yourself a favor: buy this and read it meditatively.

Mulholland, M. Robert. *Invitation to a Journey: A Road Map for Spiritual Formation.* Downers Grove, Ill.: InterVarsity Press, 1993. This book presents an understanding of Christian spiritual formation that recognizes the different ways we each approach God but also challenges us to explore spiritual disciplines with which we are less comfortable. Prayer is presented as the foundational spiritual discipline, and Mulholland's discussion of it is particularly valuable.

————. *Shaped by the Word: The Power of Scripture in Spiritual Formation.* Nashville: Upper Room, 1985. This is a straightforward and helpful discussion of how to approach the Bible with the intent of allowing ourselves to be shaped by it. Distinguishing the reading of Scripture for personal spiritual formation from other ways we can approach it, the author reminds us of the central place that God's Word should play in spiritual formation.

Narramore, Bruce. *No Condemnation.* Grand Rapids, Mich.: Zondervan, 1984. Narramore presents a fresh consideration of the biblical teaching and best psychological understandings available on the topic of guilt. He challenges the usual distinction between true and false guilt, suggesting that guilt is always destructive. Thus he suggests that in contrast to guilt, which is basically a mechanism of self-punishment, the biblical response to sin is remorse and repentance. Much more than playing with words, this book offers a helpful discussion of the nature of guilt as well as the prevalence and destructiveness of guilt motivation.

Norris, Kathleen. *The Cloister Walk.* New York: Riverhead, 1996. This *New York Times* bestseller and Notable Book of 1996 presents the spiritual autobiographical insights of a married Protestant woman who improbably found herself drawn to the ancient practice of monasticism. Her involvement in a Benedictine order provided the context for her spiritual discoveries, which are presented with grace, freshness and immediacy. Through both this book and *Amazing Grace* (1998), Norris has spoken to thousands of men and women who hear in her spiritual longings something of the stirrings of their own soul.

Nouwen, Henri. *The Inner Voice of Love.* New York: Doubleday, 1996. This is one of the most tender and moving of Nouwen's books. It was his "secret journal," written during the most difficult period of his life, when he struggled with depression and when his experience of God's love totally disappeared from his life. This is for anyone who has ever struggled spiritually or psychologically. It is a message of hope, love and faith from the heart of one who struggled deeply but whose faith in God never faltered.

———. *Reaching Out: The Three Movements of the Spiritual Life.* New York: Doubleday, 1966. This was my first encounter with Nouwen. Judging from the colors of pens and pencils used to underline in it, I would guess that I have read it at least five or six times since then. The "three movements" are from loneliness to solitude, from hostility to hospitality and from illusion to prayer. These represent ways of, respectively, reaching out to our innermost self, reaching out to other people and reaching out to God. The book is a response to the question "What does it mean to live life in the Spirit of Jesus?" Nouwen's answer to this question has made this book a modern-day spiritual classic.

————. *The Return of the Prodigal Son.* New York: Doubleday, 1994. It's difficult to limit myself to only a few books by this most loved twentieth-century Christian author and spiritual guide. But of all his books, this is the one I have reread the most often and the one that has changed my life the most significantly. It is a meditation on Rembrandt's painting *The Return of the Prodigal Son.* And that, in turn, is a meditation on the biblical parable. Nouwen uses the painting as a way to cut to the heart of the truths of this most important parable, the one many Christians over the centuries have felt contains the heart of the gospel. Read meditatively, this book holds the promise of changing your view of God forever.

————. *The Way of the Heart.* San Francisco: Harper & Row, 1981. The greatest gift many people have received from Nouwen is his help in cultivating solitude of the heart. This theme appears in the majority of his books. One book, however, is devoted exclusively to it. *The Way of the Heart* is a meditation on the contribution of desert spirituality to modern Christians. Nouwen concludes that solitude, silence and unceasing prayer form the core of the spirituality of the desert. They also offer contemporary Christians the basis for spiritual depth and vitality.

O'Donohue, John. *Eternal Echoes: Celtic Reflections on Our Yearning to Belong.* New York: HarperCollins, 1999. This book presents fresh and often profound insights on the nature of human longing, particularly the longing to belong. Although it is not written from an explicitly Christian point of view, its understanding of this essential dynamic of the soul properly captures the essential spiritual nature of this and all longings of the soul.

Packer, J. I. *Quest for Godliness.* Wheaton, Ill.: Crossway, 1994. This account of Puritan spirituality helps dispel myth and misunderstanding regarding the Puritans and places them in a light that allows their teachings to be appreciated for their value in Christian spirituality. The Puritans have much to teach us about the spiritual journey, and if you are not already directly familiar with their writings, this is as good an introduction to them as any.

Peck, M. Scott. *People of the Lie.* New York: Simon & Schuster, 1983. From my point of view, this is the most important book of this popular contemporary author. It represents a preliminary attempt to develop a psychology of evil. Rooting evil in narcissism, the author is a bit naive in his hope for its healing, but very helpful in his discussion of the relationships between narcissism, sin and evil.

Pennington, Basil M. *Centering Prayer: Renewing an Ancient Christian*

Prayer Form. New York: Image, 1982. Basil Pennington is a Trappist monk known (along with Thomas Keating) for the rediscovery of the ancient Christian approach to prayer known as centering prayer. This is his clearest expression of what this approach to prayer involves and what to expect when you learn to sit quietly before God, focusing your being upon him.

———. *Living in the Question.* New York: Continuum, 1999. This delightful little book explores what it means to live questions rather than simply seeking answers to them. The author invites the reader to meet Christ and consider some of the questions he asks his followers in the Gospels. As we do so, we are reminded of the wonderful ways that questions open up space for us to encounter God. This makes an important contribution to those who seek to accompany others on the spiritual journey.

———. *True Self/False Self.* New York: Crossroad, 2000. Presenting the false self as made up of what I have, what I do and how I want people to think of me, this book describes the bondage of such attachments and the route to freedom in Christ. According to Pennington, my true self is grounded in seeing myself reflected back in the eyes of the One who most deeply and truly loves me. We achieve this by centering ourselves in God through what Pennington calls centering prayer.

Peterson, Eugene. *Answering God: The Psalms as Tools for Prayer.* San Francisco: HarperSanFrancisco, 1989. Reading the psalms offers us a chance to listen in on the prayer life of people who knew how to be honest with their God. Peterson leads the reader into the heart of these prayer poems, offering enormous help in both understanding them and learning to make them our own. This is my favorite of the many wonderful books by this popular spiritual writer.

———. *The Contemplative Pastor: Returning to the Art of Spiritual Direction.* Dallas: Word, 1989. Here, with the freshness and immediacy that characterize his writing, Peterson calls pastors to restore spiritual direction to the heart of their ministry. This is advice from someone who has already put it into practice. The result is an encounter with the author, not simply a reading of his ideas.

Retreats Online <www.retreatsonline.com>. This website provides links to retreat centers of many different types around the world. You should select "Christian Retreats" to find the centers closest to you or wherever in the world you wish to travel.

Riso, Don Richard. *Personality Types: Using the Enneagram for Self Discovery.* Boston: Houghton Mifflin, 1987. The Enneagram is an ancient system of personality classification and understanding that has made a recent comeback in popularity thanks in large part to the prodigious writings of this author. Any of his numerous books on the approach are helpful. This one, in my opinion, is the most thorough overview, giving good background on the origins of the approach and a helpful discussion of both healthy and unhealthy manifestations of the nine basic personality types identified by this system.

―――. *Understanding the Enneagram.* Boston: Houghton Mifflin, 1990. This book is more practical and less theoretical and serves either as a nice complement to the same author's *Personality Types* or as a fine stand-alone introduction to this approach to understanding personality. In my mind, the real genius of this approach is the way it illumines the basic sin associated with each personality type. Much of the spiritual literature that has developed around the Enneagram builds on Riso's work, and this is an excellent introduction to it.

Rohr, Richard. *Everything Belongs: The Gift of Contemplative Prayer.* New York: Crossroad, 1999. This is the best book I have read on Christian spirituality in the last several years. Arguing that "spirituality is about seeing," Rohr presents contemplation as the place where we learn to live in awareness of God's presence and thereby come to see how everything fits. Never offering simply a set of prayer techniques, this book can still be fairly described as a book on prayer because its focus is increasing attunement to God and his reality. Its message is presented in the form of parables, metaphors and personal experiences. If you prefer books built on direct propositional exposition, this book is not for you. If you are open to less direct forms of exposition, it may just be for you as it has been for me—an extraordinary challenge to how I see God and his world.

Santa-Maria, Maria. *Growth Through Meditation and Journal Writing: A Jungian Perspective on Christian Spirituality.* New York: Paulist, 1983. This book offers much more than its title suggests. Although it discusses meditation and journal writing, it is really a discussion of Christian spiritual formation. There is a helpful review of the classical approaches to Christian spirituality (including a discussion of the distinctives of the understandings of spiritual formation associated with Teresa of Ávila, Ignatius of Loyola, Evelyn Underhill and Thomas Merton) as well as the author's syntheses of them in a curriculum for a nine-week spiritual formation group.

Savary, Louis, Patricia Berne and Strephon Williams. *Dreams and Spiritual Growth: A Judeo-Christian Way of Dreamwork.* New York: Paulist,

1984. This is the most helpful book I have found on the role of dreams in spiritual growth. It is eminently practical (built around thirty-seven dream-work techniques), balanced (integrating a number of diverse approaches to understanding and working with dreams) and solidly focused on spiritual formation. It will be appreciated by anyone seeking to better know their inner world and more carefully attend to God's voice in the depths of their subjectivity.

Shapiro, David. *Neurotic Styles*. New York: Basic Books, 1965. This classic discussion of four neurotic styles of functioning (obsessive-compulsive, hysterical, paranoid and impulsive) is an excellent introduction to the field of psychopathology. The approach is technical but not inaccessible to the nonspecialist with a little background in psychology. The book also serves as an excellent introduction to a psychodynamic approach to the understanding of human functioning and includes a very helpful discussion of the major mental mechanisms of defense as they operate in these neurotic styles.

Smith, James, and Lynda Graybeal. *A Spiritual Formation Workbook: Small Group Resources for Nurturing Christian Growth*. San Francisco: HarperSanFrancisco, 1999. Drawing on the six traditions of Christian spirituality described by Richard Foster in his *Streams of Living Water*, this book presents a practical and extremely helpful curriculum for the beginning stages of a spiritual formation group. The workbook is organized around nine sessions during which such a group would meet. In addition to helpful advice for the group leader, it contains a large number of exercises and discussion topics designed to aid group participants in developing a more balanced spiritual life.

Sproul, R. C. *The Holiness of God*. Wheaton, Ill.: Tyndale House, 1985. This book examines the meaning of holiness and explores why we are both fascinated and terrified by a holy God. It is a profound and spiritually edifying investigation of the dynamics of holiness as it exists in God and as it is intended to exist in us.

Sugerman, Shirley. *Sin and Madness: Studies in Narcissism*. Philadelphia: Westminster Press, 1976. Arguing that narcissism can be understood to be the core of what theologians have called sin and psychologists have called madness, this book presents an excellent exploration of the dynamics of the human tendency to pride and its self-destructiveness. These observations are offered in a nonreductionistic manner, making no attempt to suggest that sin is nothing more than either madness or narcissism. Rather, the focus is on understanding the core of egocentricity that seems to infect the souls of humans. The insights offered are helpful for anyone seeking an understanding of the dynamics of the soul.

Tan, Siang-Yang, and Douglas Gregg. *Disciplines of the Holy Spirit.* Grand Rapids, Mich.: Zondervan, 1997. Written from a mainstream evangelical perspective, this book presents attunement to the Holy Spirit as the foundation of Christian spiritual formation. The disciplines of solitude, surrender and service are seen as the core of our response to the Spirit as we draw near to God, yield to him and then reach out to others.

Teresa of Ávila. *Interior Castle.* Translated by E. A. Peers. New York: Doubleday, 1961. Teresa was an unusually gifted teacher. Her focus was the guidance of others toward spiritual perfection. *Interior Castle* deals with the development of the soul as it is progressively attuned to God. As she describes this journey, it involves moving beyond what she calls the "outward mansions" that stand in the way of the inner castle. Progress on this journey involves a deepening of one's knowledge of God and movement away from love of the world. This book is a classic of what is known as mystical theology.

Thomas à Kempis. *The Imitation of Christ.* New York: Pyramid, 1967. Widely regarded as the unchallenged masterpiece of the devotional literature of the past five hundred years, this book has helped millions of Christians draw closer to their Lord. Although some readers may find its premodern language and style somewhat arcane, it is a treasure that repays dividends to those who read it.

Tournier, Paul. *Guilt and Grace.* New York: Harper & Row, 1962. This is perhaps the finest Christian discussion of true and false guilt and the way false guilt insidiously corrodes psychological and spiritual vitality. Decades later Tournier's ideas have gained wide acceptance in North American evangelical circles, but here they are presented in one of the earliest and clearest expressions yet to be found. A valuable book about an important psychospiritual dynamic.

———. *The Meaning of Persons.* London: SCM Press, 1957. I encountered this book during my first year of university. It and Freud's *Interpretation of Dreams* formed the basis of my decision to study psychology. It is the book for which Tournier remains best known and most loved, and it remains a gem for its discussion of what it means to be a person.

———. *A Place for You.* London: SCM Press, 1968. This book is by the much-loved Swiss physician who became popular among North American Christians in the closing decades of the twentieth century. It, like all his other works, presents the gentle and warm wisdom of an astute observer of the human condition. Although Tournier was trained in psychiatry, his writings are nontechnical and highly accessible. This is my favorite of his more than twenty books. Exploring the human need to find a place we can call our own, it richly integrates psychological and spiritual dynamics. It speaks to the soul by touching our spiritual restlessness and deepest longings.

Tozer, A. W. *The Knowledge of the Holy.* New York: Harper & Row, 1961. This little book presents a meditation on the nature of God. Written as much for the heart as for the head, it breathes a spirit of devotion while establishing a sound doctrinal basis for the experience of God.

Underhill, Evelyn. *Practical Mysticism: A Little Book for Normal People.* New York: E. P. Dutton, 1943. This short introduction to Christian mysticism is written by the person who is widely recognized as the twentieth century's most important Protestant mystic. Living up to its title, it is in fact eminently practical. Defining mysticism as "the art of union with Reality," the author describes three forms of contemplation that form the core of her "method" for movement toward union with God.

Van Kaam, Adrian. *On Being Yourself: Reflections on Spirituality and Originality.* Denville, N.J.: Dimension, 1972. Written by the founding director of the Institute for Spiritual Formation at Duquesne University, this short book is a meditation on what it means to become my unique self-in-Christ. Van Kaam argues that as we become like Christ, we should not expect ourselves to become more like others; rather we should expect Christ-in-us to be a unique manifestation. However, he wisely warns about both pride and the numerous counterfeit sources of originality as he urges conformity to Christ as the only source for genuine uniqueness. More accessible than some other works of this prolific author, this little book is a gem.

Vanier, Jean. *Becoming Human.* Toronto: Anansi, 1998. Written by the founder of L'Arche, an international network of communities of intellectually disabled persons, this book presents a gripping meditation on what it means to be human and what growth in humanness involves. Imbued by the author's profound Christian faith, the result is a work that contains and synthesizes psychological and spiritual insights. Chapters on loneliness, belonging, forgiveness and inclusiveness provide the framework for Vanier's call to us to reach out to others, particularly to those who are weak and disenfranchised, if we wish to discover the Christian path to freedom and wholeness.

Vennard, Jane E. *Be Still: Designing and Leading Contemplative Retreats.* Bethesda, Md.: Alban Institute, 2000. Filled with practical suggestions about how to run a contemplative retreat, this book will be greatly appreciated by those seeking to do so. It contains helpful discussions of the role of silence, contemplative prayer, spiritual friendships, guided meditation and a number of other topics relevant to retreats and the Christian spiritual journey.

Vest, Norvene. *Gathered in the Word: Praying the Scripture in Small Groups.* Nashville: Upper Room, 1996. This is perhaps the best available contemporary resource on lectio divina, the ancient tradition of praying the Bible. It begins with a brief history of the method and quickly turns to a step-by-step strategy for employing it in groups. Highly practical and readable, this book offers help for anyone leading a retreat or running small groups.

Ware, Corinne. *Discover Your Spiritual Type: A Guide to Individual and Congregational Growth.* Bethesda, Md.: Alban Institute, 1995. This book is about discovering and developing your own way of encountering God and living in response to that experience. The author describes four basic spiritual types—head, heart, mystical and kingdom (the latter being perhaps better described as prophetic)—and outlines the strengths and weaknesses of each. The discussion of how to develop within your type reflects a helpful understanding of the role of the congregation in spiritual formation. In fact, the book is as relevant for the growth of congregational spirituality as it is for individuals.

Wesley, John. *A Plain Account of Christian Perfection.* London: Epworth, 1952. This short book presents a clear explanation of growth in Christ as growth in "perfect love." Love, according to Wesley, is intended to define our relationship to both God and others. That is the goal of Christian perfection. This book is excellent for anyone serious about his or her spiritual journey, particularly anyone who wishes to grow in love.

Willard, Dallas. *The Divine Conspiracy: Rediscovering Our Hidden Life in God.* San Francisco: HarperSanFrancisco, 1998. This book seeks to engage the reader in a fresh encounter with Christ, particularly challenging those who think they already understand him to risk a fresh hearing of his teaching. Presenting discipleship to Jesus as the very heart of the gospel, the author reminds us that "the good news for humanity is that Jesus is now taking students in the master class of life."

Index

96, 110–13, 123, 157–58,
181–83
Lawrence (Brother). *See*
Brother Lawrence
leadership, 177
lectio divina, 169–71,
177, 179–81
Lewis, C. S., 61, 66–67
listening, 158–59, 168–
71, 190–91
longings, 74, 98, 99, 103
love
demands of, 33–34
in friendship, 80
for God, 33, 123, 133
as ideal of spiritual
friendship, 65
Jesus' words about, 33
as motivation in spiri-
tual relationships, 48,
172–73, 206
for neighbor, 33–34
and obedience, 121–22
receiving God's, 33, 34,
125
and respect in mar-
riage, 186–87
and separateness, 187
in spiritual direction,
150–51
surrendering to God's,
96–97, 121–22
loyalty, 62–63, 69, 82
Loyola, Ignatius. *See* Ignatius of Loyola
Luther, Martin, 89
majesty of God, 140–41
manipulation, 75, 82, 189,
190, 195. *See also* con-
trol, absence of
marriage
becoming soul friends
before, 186
control in, 189–90
couples in spiritual
accompaniment
groups, 174–75
dialogue in, 190–92
impact of other relation-

ships on, 78–80, 81
intimacy in, 73, 187,
192–93
low expectations of,
185–86, 197–98
seeing God in spouse,
189
seeing spouse through
God's eyes, 188, 189
sexuality in, 192–94
soul friendship in, 186–
92, 197–203
soul intimacy with non-
Christian spouse, 81
spiritual direction in,
198–203, 204
spiritual friendship in,
194–98
Mary and Martha, 122–23
meditation on Scripture,
110–11, 115–17, 124,
133–34
mentoring, 28. *See also*
discipling; moral guid-
ance; spiritual direction;
spiritual formation
Merton, Thomas, 30, 38,
200
moderns, 61
Moore, Thomas, 75
moral guidance, 92
Moses, 205
Mother Teresa, 56
mutuality, 75–77
mysticism, 29–31
non-Christians, 81–82
Nouwen, Henri, 47–48
obedience, 96–97, 121–
22, 125
objectification, 55–56
O'Donohue, John, 49–50
orthodoxy, role in spiri-
tual direction, 93, 137,
155. *See also* theology
parenthood, 194–95,
199–200
passion, 66, 75, 80, 186,
191, 193
pastoral counseling, 91.

See also counseling; discipling; moral guidance;
spiritual direction
Paul (apostle), 89
Pennington, Basil, 102
Plato, 66
possessiveness, 74–75,
187, 190, 197. *See also*
jealousy
prayer
as attunement and
response to God, 94
centering, 102
contemplative, 122–23
to discern God's pres-
ence, 53–54
and dreams, 118
of head and heart, 30,
48, 122–23
as listening, 130, 131,
133
in marriage, 188–89,
199–200, 201, 202
prayer process, 94
prayerful listening, 168–
71
in spiritual accompani-
ment groups, 166, 176
in spiritual direction,
103, 104–5
and spiritual journey,
29–30
unworded, 115, 132–33
without ceasing, 106,
113, 132
preaching, 91–92
presence of God
amid trouble, 144
attending to, 52–54,
113–15, 159, 205–6
awareness of, 98–102,
130, 141
and prayer, 94
and soul intimacy, 57
in spiritual dryness,
135–39
See also examen
presence with another
person, 49–54, 158–59